CROWDFUNDING FOR ENTREPRENEURS

This is the first book of its kind to systematically integrate crowdfunding in the entrepreneurial finance research field and extend the current debate to show how crowdfunding can be leveraged as a strategic tool to grow new ventures.

Utilising original empirical evidence of companies that have raised funds via crowdfunding, it discusses the value-added services that the crowd provides to entrepreneurs, as well as how and under which conditions crowdfunding helps company development by facilitating subsequent access to critical financial and non-financial resources from external stakeholders. The first part introduces the most popular models and tactics for a successful crowdfunding campaign and illustrates the characteristics of the crowdfunding phenomenon and its evolution across the world during the last decade. The second part of the book, demonstrating how crowdfunding can be a starting point to seed financing, illustrates and discusses how entrepreneurs can use crowdfunding as a strategic tool for accessing subsequent resources from external stakeholders – showing the benefits, beyond capital, that entrepreneurs can gain from the crowd, as well as potential risks.

Crowdfunding for Entrepreneurs is particularly useful for academics, advanced undergraduate and postgraduate students in entrepreneurship and innovation, entrepreneurial finance, strategic management, as well as professionals interested in how crowdfunding can be utilised as a strategic tool to create competitive advantage.

Francesca Di Pietro is assistant professor in Business Strategy and associate director of the MSc in Entrepreneurship at Trinity Business School, Trinity College Dublin, Ireland. Her main research interests are on entrepreneurship and entrepreneurial finance. Her research has appeared in major scientific journals and books.

CROWDFUNDING FOR ENTREPRENEURS

Developing Strategic Advantage through Entrepreneurial Finance

Francesca Di Pietro

Routledge
Taylor & Francis Group
LONDON AND NEW YORK

First published 2020
by Routledge
2 Park Square, Milton Park, Abingdon, Oxon OX14 4RN

and by Routledge
52 Vanderbilt Avenue, New York, NY 10017

Routledge is an imprint of the Taylor & Francis Group, an informa business

British Library Cataloguing-in-Publication Data
A catalogue record for this book is available from the British Library

Library of Congress Cataloging-in-Publication Data
Names: Di Pietro, Francesca, 1987- author.
Title: Crowdfunding for entrepreneurs : developing strategic advantage through entrepreneurial finance / Francesca Di Pietro.
Description: Abingdon, Oxon ; New York, NY : Routledge, 2020. | Includes bibliographical references and index.
Identifiers: LCCN 2019047265 (print) | LCCN 2019047266 (ebook) | ISBN 9780367334239 (hardback) | ISBN 9780367334253 (paperback) | ISBN 9780429319785 (ebook)
Subjects: LCSH: Crowd funding. | Venture capital.
Classification: LCC HG4751 .D495 2020 (print) | LCC HG4751 (ebook) | DDC 658.15/224--dc23
LC record available at https://lccn.loc.gov/2019047265
LC ebook record available at https://lccn.loc.gov/2019047266

ISBN: 978-0-367-33423-9 (hbk)
ISBN: 978-0-367-33425-3 (pbk)
ISBN: 978-0-429-31978-5 (ebk)

Typeset in Bembo
by Lumina Datamatics Limited

CONTENTS

PART II
Deciphering equity crowdfunding 61

FIGURES

Colour images are available online at https://www.routledge.com/Crowdfunding-for-Entrepreneurs-Developing-Strategic-Advantage-through/Pietro/p/book/9780367334253.

TABLES

ACRONYMS

3Fs	Friends, Family and Fools
B2C	Business-to-Consumer
CTO	Chief Technology Office
CVC	Corporate Venture Capital
EIS	Enterprise Investment Scheme
EVS	European Value Survey
FCA	Financial Conduct Authority
GEM	Global Entrepreneurship Monitor
ICT	Information and Communication Technologies
IP	Intellectual Property
IPO	Initial Public Offering
IPR	Intellectual Property Rights
LAC	Latin American Countries
MD	Managing Director
P2P	Peer-to-Peer
SEC	Securities and Exchange Commission
SEIS	Seed Enterprise Investment Scheme
SMEs	Small and Medium-Sized Enterprises
TEA	Total Entrepreneurship Activity
UK	United Kingdom
US	United States
VC	Venture Capital
VCs	Venture Capitalists
WDI	World Development Indicators

1

INTRODUCTION TO THE BOOK

Crowdfunding, as a source of early finance, has attracted increasing interest from economists, management scholars, and political scientists concerned about its impact on entrepreneurial activities. Over the past 5 years, a great deal of research has been published on crowdfunding, from a range of perspectives.

The goal of the present book is to systematically integrate crowdfunding in the entrepreneurial finance literature and extend current debate on crowdfunding to include how it can become a strategic tool for entrepreneurs, to develop and grow their ventures and provide vital access to finance.

The chapters in this book focus on the post-funding phase of equity crowd financing. Relying on original qualitative and quantitative empirical evidence on UK firms that have searched for equity crowdfunding, this book provides insights into the value-added provided by crowd investors after the initial fundraising event and the post-funding performance of crowdfunded firms.

The book is organised in two parts that address interrelated topics. Following this introductory chapter, the first part of the book, Chapters 2–4, describes crowdfunding and the most popular crowdfunding models. It offers an up-to-date account of the relevant research findings and analyses the geography of crowdfunding, including fundraising patterns worldwide.

Chapter 2 introduces the concept of entrepreneurial finance, differentiating among the stages of new venture development, and the available sources of finance. It presents the crowdfunding phenomenon and provides a classification of the most popular crowdfunding types and a description of the three main actors in the crowdfunding process. In the context of these actors (firm creator, funders, and crowdfunding platform), the focus is on creators' and funders' incentives and disincentives, in the former case for seeking crowdfunding and in the latter case for deciding to invest. The chapter concludes by outlining the steps in the crowdfunding fundraising process.

Chapter 3 provides a more detailed picture of crowdfunding and a review of current work on the factors associated to fundraising success, across different crowdfunding models.

Chapter 4 presents and compares the evolution of crowdfunding around the world, examining three specific markets – Europe, America, and Asia-Pacific. It explores the effects of formal institutions, such as legal frameworks, and informal institutions, such as culture, on differences in the adoption and development of crowdfunding across European countries.

The second part of the book, Chapters 5–7, focuses on equity crowdfunding. Drawing on original qualitative and quantitative data on equity crowd-funded companies in the UK, this part of the book investigates the value-added services provided by crowd investors. It considers crowdfunding as initial seed funding and describes and discusses whether and under what conditions equity crowdfunding facilitates entrepreneurs' performance and subsequent access to external financial resources.

Chapter 5 opens with a detailed description of the equity crowdfunding phenomenon in Europe and an in-depth analysis of the two most popular platforms in the UK, Crowdcube and Seedrs, to highlight their main differences. Next, drawing on original qualitative data on UK companies that have used equity crowdfunding, Chapter 5 discusses the advantages and disadvantages of this form of funding, from the point of view of both entrepreneurs and investors.

Chapter 6 provides an up-to-date review of the literature on equity crowdfunding and examines the post-funding phase and how entrepreneurs can leverage the crowd to obtain additional, non-financial benefits such as knowledge and networks.

Chapter 7 reviews the most recent research on the performance of crowdfunded companies and how this form of funding enabled access to additional finance. It provides empirical evidence on the performance of crowd-backed companies in the UK, based on data on over 200 companies that were successful in obtaining equity crowdfunding.

Chapter 7 concludes the book with some final reflections and suggestions for future research on this new exciting topic.

PART I

Crowdfunding: understanding the phenomenon

The first part of this book provides a general introduction to crowdfunding. Chapter 1 introduces the book and provides a brief description of the key topics covered in each book chapter. Chapter 2 introduces the concept of entrepreneurial finance, differentiating among the stages of new venture development and the sources of finance available. Chapter 3 provides a state-of-the-art review of current research on crowdfunding, highlighting the success factors related to crowdfunding campaigns. Chapter 4 investigates adoption of crowdfunding across Europe, America, and Asia-Pacific regions, looking at explanations for differences linked to formal institutions such as legal framework, or informal institutions such as culture.

2

FINANCE FOR ENTREPRENEURSHIP

An introduction

This chapter reviews the alternative sources of financing available to entrepreneurs, highlighting their differences and their roles in the financing cycle for new ventures. It provides a description and general overview of the crowdfunding phenomenon, the different crowdfunding types in use, such as donation, reward, lending, and equity crowdfunding, and actors and stages in the fundraising process.

2.1 Entrepreneurial finance landscape

Entrepreneurial finance is a recently emerged research field, positioned at the intersection between entrepreneurship and finance. The notion of entrepreneurship dates back to 1775 when Richard Cantillon defined an entrepreneur as an "adventurer," as someone willing to take risks and act under uncertainty (Cantillon, 1775). Subsequent research, building on Cantillon's work, defined an entrepreneur as an individual able to recognise and exploit opportunities available to everyone (Kirzner, 1973). Schumpeter defined an entrepreneur as an innovator, involved in "the doing of new things or the doing of things that are already being done in a new way" (Schumpeter, 1947: 151). These various definitions all refer to entrepreneurship as involving recognition of an opportunity and the steps related to transforming the opportunity or idea into a reality. To embark on an entrepreneurial endeavour requires resources and their acquisition has attracted a great deal of research attention in the field of entrepreneurship (see, e.g. Alvarez and Busenitz, 2001; Alvarez and Barney, 2007; Hellmann and Puri, 2002; West and Noel, 2009). Resources are a basic condition for entrepreneurship (Kirzner, 1997; Barney, 1986). Whether tangible or intangible, resources are required for the creation of economic wealth associated to a market opportunity (Barney, 1986; Penrose, 1959). Therefore, lack of the resources required to exploit an opportunity makes access to external sources critical (Alvarez and

Barney, 2007; Colombo et al., 2006). Initially, the entrepreneur may have fairly scant knowledge about the environment, lack employees' commitment and relationships with customers and suppliers (Stinchcombe, 1965). The building of competitive advantage requires an ability to access external sources to overcome these constraints (Dyer and Singh, 1998; Grant and Baden-Fuller, 2004; Yli-Renko et al., 2001; Autio et al., 2000; West and Noel, 2009).

Among the most important resources is money. It is well known that one of the main problems faced by entrepreneurs in the early stage of a business initiative, is how to attract external financial investment (see, e.g. Colombo and Grilli, 2010; Hellmann and Puri, 2002; Cosh et al., 2009). Research on entrepreneurial finance examines how entrepreneurs garner the required financial resources and identifies the advantages and disadvantages of different sources of finance at different stages of the new venture's life cycle. Entrepreneurial finance tends to involve mainly private rather than public funding. This private funding can come from family and friends, incubators and accelerators, crowd funders, business angels, venture capitalists, and banks (Alemany and Andreoli, 2018). These sources may play a broader role in the start-up companies they finance through the provision of business advice, experience, and connections (see, e.g. Hellmann and Puri, 2002; Gilson, 2003; Sapienza et al., 1996; Colombo and Grilli, 2010). Finance, in fact, is not the only resource necessary for start-up success.

Entrepreneurial finance is relevant both to establish the new company and to support the various stages of development of the entrepreneurial project. Depending on the stage of development, financial and strategic exigencies assume different importance. In this book, we consider four different development stages, which are depicted in Figure 2.1. Figure 2.1 indicates the most typical sources of funding in each stage.[1]

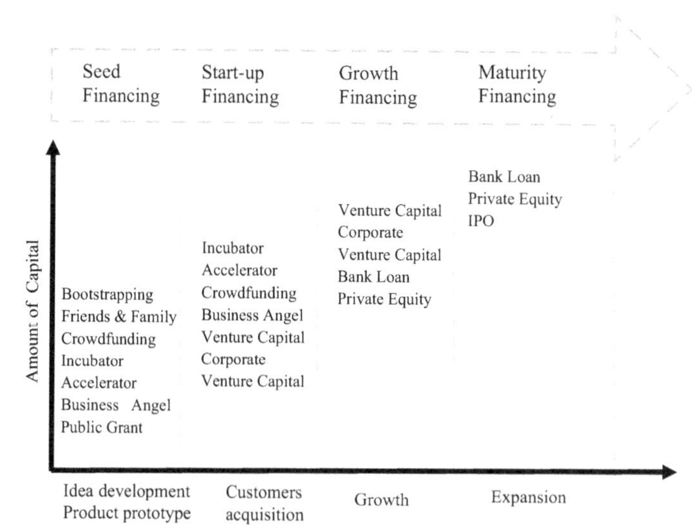

FIGURE 2.1 Source of funding by venture development stage

2.1.1 Seed financing

Seed financing is required in the first phase of the new venture lifecycle. In most cases, this is before the company has been established and refers to identification of a business idea, which the entrepreneur is keen to invest time and resources to its development. This phase may involve the development of a first product or service prototype to test the market and identify who might be willing to pay for the product or service.

Depending on the type ofbusiness, the founder will need some funding. The firm founder's initial source of finance will be entrepreneur's own resources, employed through a process known as "bootstrapping" (Freear et al., 1995; Harrison et al., 2004), plus contributions from friends and family, which have been described as "love capital" or Friends, Family, and Fools (3Fs) financing. 3Fs financing is provided by those with close links to the founding team, who have faith in their ability to execute the project. In this seed phase, research grants and other public funds are other important sources of funding. Crowdfunding, incubators and accelerators, and business angels may provide finance and other support for the new company.

Crowdfunding, which is described later in this book, allows the entrepreneur to gather online financing from the crowd via a dedicated platform (Belleflamme et al., 2014). Incubators and accelerators are a relatively recent type of support which is spreading quite quickly. Incubators provide new, small ventures with resources (Allen and McCluskey, 1991) that improve their chances of successful firm foundation (Löfsten and Lindelöf, 2002; Hackett and Dilts, 2008; Dettwiler et al., 2006). Incubators also increase the probability of firm survival (Schwartz, 2009, 2013) and accelerate their development (Mian, 1997). Business incubators support nascent companies and entrepreneurs until the business becomes sustainable (Lalkaka and Bishop, 1996). They provide physical facilities and intangible valuable assets including, among others, management and legal services, and networking opportunities (Aernoudt, 2004; Tötterman and Sten, 2005; Hughes et al., 2007; Soetanto and Jack, 2013).

Although both incubators and accelerators help to boost innovation, they differ in certain important ways. Accelerators focus on scaling up the business and accelerating the growth of an existing company, while incubators provide support before the foundation of the firm. They may support the development of a disruptive idea and design of a business model allowing company formation. Accelerators provide support over a fixed-term (usually three months) and may offer mentoring and training, equity capital, and space (Cohen and Hochberg, 2014; Hochberg, 2016; Cohen, 2013). Accelerator and incubator services have some overlaps. Both provide active support for start-ups through the provision of technology, market and financial knowledge, advice and mentoring, and changes to increase the entrepreneur's network (Bruneel et al., 2012; Pauwels et al., 2016). They provide services from and contacts with other entrepreneurs, sector experts, and professionals, all of which may be the source of strategic and managerial advice and help related to obtaining additional finance.

Business angels are high-net-worth individuals who invest their capital, time, and expertise in a business (Kelly, 2007). Most business angel investors are experienced entrepreneurs (Gaston, 1989; Hindle and Lee, 2002; Wright et al., 1998; Aernoudt, 1999) who expect high returns from their investments. Angel investors are described sometimes as "mentor capitalists" (Leonard and Swap, 2000) since they tend to expect to play an active role in the companies in which they invest, and to provide knowledge, expertise, mentoring, and act as sounding boards for the entrepreneur (Croce et al., 2017; Ehrlich et al., 1994; Mason and Harrison, 1996; Brettel, 2003; Madill et al., 2005; Matlay and Sørheim, 2005; Freear et al., 1995). In the seed phase, most entrepreneurs are seeking an amount of funding less than €1 million.

2.1.2 Start-up financing

In the start-up phase, the company is already involved in selling its products or services. The start-up phase continues until breakeven is achieved (Barringer and Ireland, 2006) and the firm is able to cover its operating costs. Winning the first customer is an important milestone and is a validation of the business concept. However, the goal is to grow the customer base and develop and apply an efficient plan to scale-up the business. In this start-up phase, depending on the firm's financial needs, the best suitable source of funding is business angels or venture capital (Jeng and Wells, 2000; Zider, 1998). Venture capitalists (VCs) are financial intermediaries who raise money from individuals and institutions for investment in private companies that offer high potential, but also high risk (Zider, 1998).

A venture capital (VC) firm will manage several pools of capital and invest in a broad range of industries, not just high technology start-ups. In general, if the amount required is greater than €1 million, venture capital will be the most appropriate source.

VCs assist business development start-ups in various ways (see, e.g. Colombo and Grilli, 2010; Bertoni et al., 2011; Bottazzi et al., 2008; Croce et al., 2013), which can include mentoring, financial assistance (Hellmann and Puri, 2002; Stuart et al., 1999), recruiting senior staff (Gorman and Sahlman, 1989; Hellmann and Puri, 2002), and facilitating access to external resources that otherwise would be beyond the reach of the start-up (Colombo et al., 2006; Hsu, 2006). Research shows that VC investor involvement can benefit the development of venture capital backed companies, (Bertoni et al., 2011; Colombo and Murtinu, 2017; Cumming et al., 2017) which implies that they provide value added to the firm that goes beyond provision of financial capital.

The venture capital is used to fund firm growth in order to maximise financial returns from existing investments by selling the firm or through an Initial Public Offering (IPO). VCs allow access to large networks of industry players and other actors, which increase the chances of obtaining further funding (Hsu, 2004) and can increase firm performance (Bottazzi et al., 2008; Croce et al., 2013; Jackson et al., 2012).

Lastly, large corporations may contribute to start-up financing. Corporations are interested in acquiring new technology and investing in young companies based on provision of corporate venture capital (CVC) (Dushnitsky, 2012; Chesbrough, 2002). Big corporations often invest in firms producing goods linked to their business, in order to keep abreast of the latest trends and technologies. This investment can take various forms such as an accelerator programme or an in-house VC activity (Hill and Birkinshaw, 2008; Dushnitsky, 2012; Souitaris and Zerbinati, 2014). Corporate investors supply valuable complementary non-pecuniary resources and capabilities to the ventures they invest in (Block and MacMillan, 1993; Chesbrough, 2000), in return for both direct monetary benefits and indirect strategic benefits (Dushnitsky and Lenox, 2006). This type of investment is more frequent in the USA than in Europe.

2.1.3 Growth financing

In the growth financing phase, the firm's sales continue to grow, the entrepreneurial activity slows, and the firm becomes profitable. Most of this profit is invested in further growth such as the launch of new products lines and entry to new markets. Growth is the main driver of the business. In this stage, long-term funding is required, which requires a good track record of successful firm operation to attract financial partners such as VC, private equity, and commercial banks.

Similar to venture capital, private equity funds come from investors that provide capital to non-listed companies in exchange for company shares. Private equity funds are managed by large institutional investors and wealthy individuals and are invested in mature companies operating in traditional sectors with proven business models, that are trying to expand their businesses locally or internationally, or consolidate their activities through a merger, acquisition, or other corporate transaction (Alemany and Andreoli, 2018).

2.1.4 Maturity financing

In this stage, the company has reached a phase where sales have stabilised due to a high level of competition and market saturation. The company's main goal is to maintain its market share and, perhaps, enter new markets with innovations that will make it more competitive. Private equity and initial public offerings (IPOs) are the main sources of financing in this stage. An IPO occurs with the first offer of the firm's stock to the public and the listing of its shares on the stock market. Following an IPO, the company's shares can be traded freely on the stock market and the company becomes a public company. For private investors, such as VC or private equity funds, an IPO is the preferred route to exit for the best-performing ventures (Mason and Harrison, 2002; Achleitner et al., 2013).

2.2 Introduction to crowdfunding

Crowdfunding can be defined as "an open call, essentially through the internet, for the provision of financial resources in order to support initiatives for specific purposes" (Schwienbacher and Larralde, 2010). Mollick (2014) defines crowdfunding in an entrepreneurial context as the efforts of an individual entrepreneur or a group of entrepreneurs to fund their ventures by drawing on relatively small-sized contributions from a relatively large number of funders, using the Internet. The crowdfunding phenomenon is part of a broader trend toward mobilising the crowd for various purposes including crowdsourcing, which refers to the practice of inviting large groups to contribute to projects, share ideas or co-develop software and other products via the Internet (Baldwin and Von Hippel, 2011). Crowdsourcing leverages information technology-based mobilisation of new ideas and solutions to problems, from a geographically dispersed pool of potential contributors (Chesbrough, 2006).

Crowdfunding focuses on micro-finance (Morduch, 1999) and is a unique form of fundraising. The modern crowdfunding phenomenon has a basis in eighteenth and nineteenth century practices (Calveri and Esposito, 2013), the most famous example being when, in 1884, the American Committee for the Statue of Liberty ran out of funding for the pedestal and sought public donations. Joseph Pulitzer, publisher of the *New York World* newspaper, decided to support this search for funding and established a goal of $100,000, to be raised by every reader donating $US1 in exchange for a six-inch-high reproduction of the statue. The results were astonishing; in less than six months the $US100,000 goal was reached on 11 August 1885.

Today, crowdfunding is facilitated by technology. The diffusion of information and communication technologies (ICT) has provided an infrastructure allowing access to millions of people and potential investors across the world. The general social acceptance of technology-enabled social networks has enabled the building of trust among people with whom they have few traditional connections. The development of Web 2.0 technologies has facilitated interactions via the Internet, the 2008 global financial crisis has made bank credit more expensive and less accessible to start-up companies, and the popularity of crowdsourcing, also, has contributed to the development of the crowdfunding phenomenon (Agrawal et al., 2015).

Crowdfunding is examplary of a two-sided market which links two different groups of users within a network (Eisenmann et al., 2009). These users are

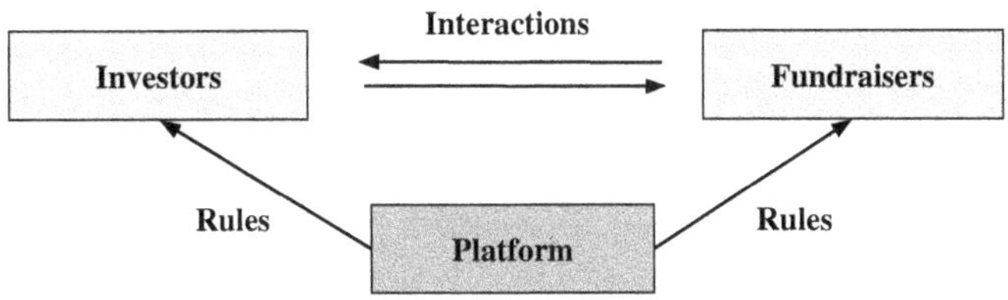

FIGURE 2.2 Crowdfunding: a two-side market

connected via a digital market place or website to exchange funds. A two-sided market typically involves three distinct activities; the crowd or the backers, the project proponent, and the platform (see Figure 2.2). The crowdfunding platform acts as the intermediary between investors and fundraisers, both of which are subject to the rules implemented by the crowdfunding platform.

2.2.1 The fundraiser

The fundraiser, who promotes a project via the platform, may be an individual, a group of individuals, or an organisation. Individual fundraisers often describe themselves as entrepreneurs in order to collect funds to develop their business ideas (Jian and Shin, 2015).

The literature proposes several reasons to understand the reasons fundraisers decide to use crowdfunding instead of traditional funding methods (e.g. Gerber et al., 2012; Harms, 2007). Start-ups and small entrepreneurs consider crowdfunding to be an alternative way to access funding and overcome the barriers related to traditional funding methods. In addition to obtaining financing, crowdfunding provides some idea of the market for their products, based on the willingness to contribute (Belleflamme et al., 2014). Crowdfunding allows advance payment to support the production phase (Gerber et al., 2012) and demonstrate to traditional financial investors that there is a demand for the product (Mollick, 2014). Crowdfunding is also a marketing tool (Mollick and Kuppuswamy, 2014), since it publicises and increases awareness of the project to individuals beyond the fundraisers immediate social network.

Lastly, crowdfunding allows the fundraiser to evaluate his or her managerial ability without exchanges of equity entailing loss of control and dilution costs.

2.2.2 Investors

Investors (or backers) engage in the crowdfunding campaign by providing financial and other types of support. There are several monetary and non-monetary motivations for backers to engage in crowdfunding. Non-monetary motivations include, but are not limited to, desire to collect external rewards such as: acknowledgment; a tangible artefact or experience; participation in a community (Gerber et al., 2012); provision of help to allow others to realise their goals (philanthropic behaviour); and obtain social recognition (Colombo et al., 2015). A genuine interest in the proposed project is a huge motivator of provision of backing via a crowdfunding campaign. In many cases, backers form the company's initial customers base and contribute to the development and design of the product (Gerber et al., 2012; Di Pietro et al., 2018). Another incentive for participation in a crowdfunding campaign is economic return. This is especially relevant in the case of equity-based and lending-based models (described in the paragraph 2.3), where the economic benefits linked to company performance are obtained in exchange for contribution.

2.2.3 The platform

Crowdfunding platforms are intermediaries that enable transactions between fundraisers and investors. The platforms enable one-to-many connections and allow online communities that assist the fundraiser to develop the project (Hagiu and Wright, 2014). The platform establishes rules related to exchanges and interactions between investors and fundraisers. The related transaction fees are paid by the fundraiser depending on the amount raised and only in the case of a successful campaign. In most cases, it is costless for investors to invest in a project.

Platforms are designed on the basis of two different funding mechanisms: (i) an all-or-nothing funding approach where the project proponent receives funding only if the full target is achieved; otherwise, the investors have their investment refunded (Cumming et al., 2015; Haas et al., 2014); and (ii) a keep-it-all funding approach where the project proponent receives whatever amount is collected.

2.3 Investment and non-investment crowdfunding models

Crowdfunding has no unique form; the phenomenon has several variations whose number varies among different studies.[2] However, most research classifies it into four types, depending on the crowd funders' rights to the project outcome.

We can distinguish between investment and non-investment funding models. Non-investment funding includes donations-based and rewards-based funding where the backers do not receive any monetary benefit from supporting a crowdfunding campaign. The investment model includes lending-based and equity-based crowdfunding where the backers receive some monetary return from their crowdfunding investment.

Below we present the four funding models to explore their characteristics. Figure 2.3 depicts the main crowdfunding models.

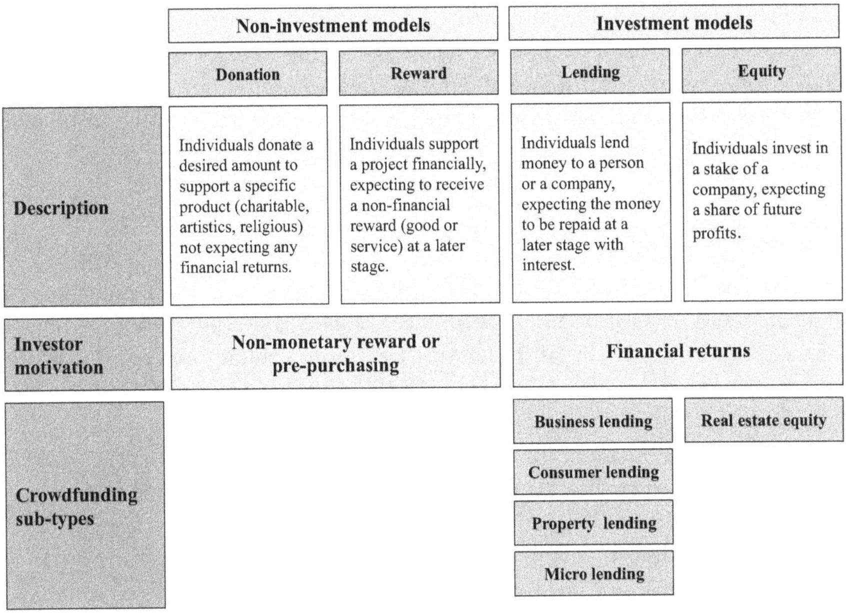

FIGURE 2.3 Investment and non-investment crowdfunding models

2.3.1 *Non-investment crowdfunding models*

2.3.1.1 *Donation-based crowdfunding*

Donation-based crowdfunding allows individuals (donors) to finance individual or company projects, in exchange for non-monetary benefits based on philanthropic or civic motivations. Donation-based crowdfunding models are generally used to support social-oriented projects, humanitarian projects, or individual creative projects, proposed by community-based organisations, non-profit organisations, or creative enterprises (Di Pietro et al., 2019). The fundraiser's personal connections and the support from his or her local community play a major part in the success of a donation-based crowdfunding campaign.

The US-based GoFundMe platform is one of the most well-known donation-based platforms worldwide. The platform was launched in 2010 and has been used by tens of millions of donors and has raised over $US5 billion for the various crowdfunding campaigns it has hosted. GoFundMe allows users to create their own website to appeal for money. This allows them to describe the fundraising cause and detail the amount required; they can upload photos or videos and share the project with the individuals in their social networks. Individuals can donate to the user via the website and leave comments in support of the project. Donation-based platforms charge very small transaction fees (less than 5% of the amount collected); if no donations are received, no charge is levied.

There are many other donation-based platforms who operate locally and worldwide, in different countries, such as JustGiving in the UK, Iodono.com in Italy. In Germany, for instance about 150 platforms allow some form of donation-based crowdfunding. Most of these platforms are very small and operate only in a small region (Ziegler et al., 2018).

2.3.1.2 Reward-based crowdfunding

Backers provide finance to individuals, projects, or companies in exchange for non-monetary rewards. The most frequent reward is pre-purchase of products or services (Gerber et al., 2012) but they can also be public acknowledgements, an artist's autograph, acknowledgement in the credits to an artistic production, a tee-shirt, etc. (Kuppuswamy and Bayus, 2017).

Reward-based financing is geared toward start-ups, particularly in creative fields, that do not qualify for traditional small-business loans, but may have a compelling project or a need to test whether there is a potential market. Reward-based crowdfunding is particular useful for start-ups in the very early-stage of development when they need seed finance. Funders can be considered early customers, who have the possibility to receive the product before it is generally available, and at a lower price (Mollick, 2014). The best-known platforms hosting this type of funding are Kickstarter and Indiegogo, which are based in the US, but operate worldwide; numerous other platforms operate locally. Anyone can contribute – family, friends, customers, business partners – to a reward crowdfunding campaign. Individual contributions may be small, so business owners need to persuade as many people as possible to participate. The platform charges a percentage, which can be as low as 5% or as high as 13% of the funds raised and may charge an additional processing fee.

2.3.2 Investment crowdfunding models

2.3.2.1 Lending-based crowdfunding

Lending-based crowdfunding emerged in early 2006 in the US, and a few years earlier in Europe, in the UK. Lending-based or peer-to-peer (P2P) lending, allows individuals to borrow money from the crowd and pay it back with interest. Interest rates are high enough to generate good returns for investors (assuming sufficient diversification of their loan portfolios) and, potentially, better than from traditional money markets or bonds. The lending-based crowdfunding process is generally a faster way to obtain money compared to traditional lenders. Transaction fees and interest rates on loans depend on the borrower's credit risk. Lending-based crowdfunding is best suited to firms in the growth stage, with a viable product that has gone through a few iterations and some initial revenue, which allows the firm to offer tangible rewards such as monetary interest (Paschen, 2017; Kgoroeadira et al., 2019).

In P2P consumer lending, funders -either individuals or institutions- provide small loans to a borrower for his or her own personal use; in P2P business lending, funders provide a loan to a business borrower. Zopa is one of the biggest lending platforms in Europe and was the first P2P lending platform for consumers in the UK. Funding Circle and Assetz Capital are other lending platforms based in the UK. The US Lending Club was launched in 2006 in San Francisco; Prosper is another well-known US lending platform.

Micro-lending is a form of lending-based crowdfunding that allows low-income clients to obtain finance. This group includes private consumers and workers who do not have easy access to banking and other financial services. Kiva, US-based, is the biggest platform in the micro-funding market.

2.3.2.2 Equity-based crowdfunding

Equity crowdfunding provides an opportunity for ventures to obtain funding from a wide range of investors, in exchange for some of the firm's equity (Ahlers et al., 2015). Equity funders become fully fledged company shareholders, and, thus, the return on their investment is linked to firm performance.

Involvement of the company's share transactions and the risk this implies, imposes some constraints on the diffusion of equity crowdfunding in Europe and the US. In particular, regulators, based on the financial sophistication of crowd investors, imposed transaction limits of private companies' shares.

In Europe, the equity crowdfunding market is most developed and is largest in the UK (Ziegler et al., 2018, 2019). The UK is considered the crowdfunding leader in Europe and is significant from an international perspective. The UK has embraced and welcomed alternative funding channels and allowed thousands of people to obtain returns from money invested in small start-ups. The two most active UK platforms are Crowdcube[3] and Seedrs,[4] which were founded respectively in 2009 and 2011. In the rest of Europe there are several other equity-funding platforms such as Seedmatch (Germany), Wiseed (France), Symbid (Netherlands), and FoundedByMe (Sweden).

Accredited and non-accredited investors[5] can participate in equity crowdfunding projects. Accredited investors include banks, insurance companies, employee benefit plans and trusts, and sufficiently wealthy and financially sophisticated individuals who have less need for protection of their investments. UK and US regulation imposes restrictions on how much non-accredited investors can invest during a 12-month period, based on their self-certified net worth and income. In Chapter 5, we explore equity crowdfunding and related regulation in more detail.

2.4 The fundraising process in crowdfunding

To better understand how equity crowdfunding works in practice, we describe the process that entrepreneurs and individuals need to follow. Figure 2.4 presents the four main steps to raising funds online via a platform.

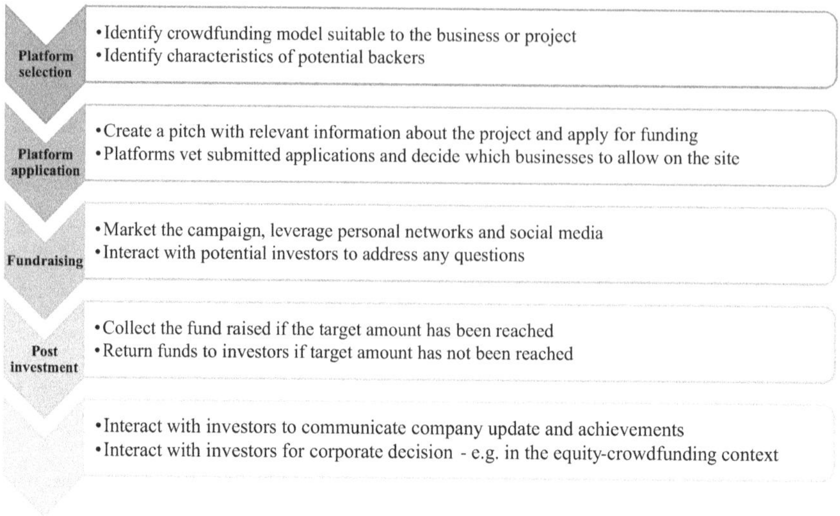

FIGURE 2.4 Entrepreneur fundraising process in crowdfunding

2.4.1 Platform selection

Before launching a start-up idea, product, service, or project, the entrepreneur must identify the most appropriate platform and crowdfunding model. Current crowdfunding sites have different-sized audiences, demographics, and campaign options. To be confident in the choice of platform requires extensive research and a good understanding of the target market. The entrepreneur must understand his or her potential backers and tailor the campaign accordingly.

2.4.2 Platform application

After identifying a platform, the entrepreneur must design the crowdfunding campaign and submit it to due diligence conducted by the platform to ensure it is fair, clear, and meets the platform's requirements. Once the due diligence process has been completed, the campaign or "pitch" can go live.[6]

2.4.3 Fundraising

The entrepreneur then needs to obtain the support of his or her broad network via social media, to ensure that the proposal has a good reach. The average length of a campaign is 60 days, during which time it is important that the entrepreneur interacts with would be investors, responds to questions or doubts, and provides additional information on the company or the project when requested.

2.4.4 Post-investment

At the end of fundraising period, the entrepreneur will (or not) collect the funds raised, depending on the platform's funding approach – all-or-nothing of keep-it-all – described previously. Interactions between crowd funders and investors continue after the fundraising campaign finishes; the extent of their relationship depends strictly on how active or passive the funders choose to be and the willingness of the entrepreneur to engage with the crowd.

Notes

1 Depending on the focus, there may be alternative classifications of the venture development stages; here we focus on finance.
2 There are different classifications and sub-categories of crowdfunding; here we consider the four main ones. For a more detailed classification, see the European Taxonomy in the 4th European Alternative Finance Benchmarking Report (Ziegler et al., 2019).
3 www.crowdcube.com.
4 www.seedrs.com.
5 For more information see: https://www.investor.gov/additional-resources/news-alerts/alerts-bulletins/updated-investor-bulletin-accredited-investors.
6 Pitch can be categorised as "elevator," a "video" or "business" and refers to the concise and attractive delivery of business plan verbally. In crowdfunding the delivery is performed as video or text description tracing not only the business model, but also founders' background, investment amount, and its intended use.

References

Achleitner, A.K., Engel, N. and Reiner, U., 2013. The performance of venture capital investments: Do investors overreact? *Review of Financial Economics*, *22*(1), pp. 20–35.

Aernoudt, R., 1999. Business angels: Should they fly on their own wings? *Venture Capital: An International Journal of Entrepreneurial Finance*, *1*(2), pp. 187–195.

Aernoudt, R., 2004. Incubators: Tool for entrepreneurship? *Small Business Economics*, *23*(2), pp. 127–135.

Agrawal, A., Catalini, C. and Goldfarb, A., 2015. Crowdfunding: Geography, social networks, and the timing of investment decisions. *Journal of Economics & Management Strategy*, *24*(2), pp. 253–274.

Ahlers, G.K., Cumming, D., Günther, C. and Schweizer, D., 2015. Signaling in equity crowdfunding. *Entrepreneurship Theory and Practice*, *39*(4), pp. 955–980.

Alemany, L. and Andreoli, J.J. eds., 2018. *Entrepreneurial Finance: The Art and Science of Growing Ventures*. Cambridge University Press.

Allen, D.N. and McCluskey, R., 1991. Structure, policy, services, and performance in the business incubator industry. *Entrepreneurship Theory and Practice*, *15*(2), pp. 61–77.

Alvarez, S. and Barney, J.B., 2007. The entrepreneurial theory of the firm. *Journal of Management Studies*, *44*(7), pp. 1057–1063.

Alvarez, S.A. and Busenitz, L.W., 2001. The entrepreneurship of resource-based theory. *Journal of Management*, *27*(6), pp. 755–775.

Autio, E., Sapienza, H.J. and Almeida, J.G., 2000. Effects of age at entry, knowledge intensity, and imitability on international growth. *Academy of Management Journal*, *43*(5), pp. 909–924.

Baldwin, C.Y. and Von Hippel, E., 2011. Modeling a paradigm shift: From producer innovation to user and open collaborative innovation. *Organization Science, 22*(6), pp. 1399–1417.

Barney, J.B., 1986. Strategic factor markets: Expectations, luck, and business strategy. *Management Science, 32*(10), pp. 1231–1241.

Barringer, B.R. and Ireland, R.D., 2006. *Entrepreneurship: Successfully Launching New Ventures.* Pearson Education India, Upper Saddle River, NJ.

Belleflamme, P., Lambert, T. and Schwienbacher, A., 2014. Crowdfunding: Tapping the right crowd. *Journal of Business Venturing, 29*(5), pp. 585–609.

Bertoni, F., Colombo, M.G. and Grilli, L., 2011. Venture capital financing and the growth of high-tech start-ups: Disentangling treatment from selection effects. *Research Policy, 40*(7), pp. 1028–1043.

Block, Z. and MacMillan, I., 1993. *Corporate Venturing: Creating New Businesses within the Firm.* Harvard Business School Press, Boston, MA.

Bottazzi, L., Da Rin, M. and Hellmann, T., 2008. Who are the active investors? *Journal of Financial Economics, 3*(89), pp. 488–512.

Brettel, M., 2003. Business angels in Germany: A research note. *Venture Capital, 5*(3), pp. 251–268.

Bruneel, J., Ratinho, T., Clarysse, B. and Groen, A., 2012. The evolution of business incubators: Comparing demand and supply of business incubation services across different incubator generations. *Technovation, 32*(2), pp. 110–121.

Calveri, C. and Esposito, R., 2013. Crowdfunding World 2013: Report, analysis & trends. DeRev. https://www.fundraisingschool.it/wp-content/uploads/2014/06/Crowdfunding-World-2013-Report-analisi-e-trend.pdf

Cantillon, R., 1775. The circulation and exchange of goods and merchandise. *Essai sur la Nature du Commerce en Général.*

Chesbrough, H., 2000. Designing corporate ventures in the shadow of private venture capital. *California Management Review, 42*(3), pp. 31–49.

Chesbrough, H., 2006. Open innovation: A new paradigm for understanding industrial innovation. In Chesbrough, H., Vanhaverbeke, W. and West, J. (eds.), *Open Innovation: Researching a New Paradigm.* Oxford University Press, Oxford, UK.

Chesbrough, H.W., 2002. Making sense of corporate venture capital. *Harvard Business Review, 80*(3), pp. 90–99.

Cohen, S., 2013. What do accelerators do? Insights from incubators and angels. *Innovations: Technology, Governance, Globalization, 8*(3–4), pp. 19–25.

Cohen, S. and Hochberg, Y.V., 2014. Accelerating startups: The seed accelerator phenomenon. Available at https://ssrn.com/abstract=2418000 or http://dx.doi.org/10.2139/ssrn.2418000.

Colombo, M.G. and Grilli, L., 2010. On growth drivers of high-tech start-ups: Exploring the role of founders' human capital and venture capital. *Journal of Business Venturing, 25*(6), pp. 610–626.

Colombo, M.G., Franzoni, C. and Rossi-Lamastra, C., 2015. Internal social capital and the attraction of early contributions in crowdfunding. *Entrepreneurship Theory and Practice, 39*(1), pp. 75–100.

Colombo, M.G., Grilli, L. and Piva, E., 2006. In search of complementary assets: The determinants of alliance formation of high-tech start-ups. *Research Policy, 35*(8), pp. 1166–1199.

Colombo, M.G. and Murtinu, S., 2017. Venture capital investments in Europe and portfolio firms' economic performance: Independent versus corporate investors. *Journal of Economics & Management Strategy, 26*(1), pp. 35–66.

Cosh, A., Cumming, D. and Hughes, A., 2009. Outside enterpreneurial capital. *The Economic Journal, 119*(540), pp. 1494–1533.

Croce, A., Martí, J. and Murtinu, S., 2013. The impact of venture capital on the productivity growth of European entrepreneurial firms: "Screening" or "value added" effect? *Journal of Business Venturing, 28*(4), pp. 489–510.

Croce, A., Tenca, F. and Ughetto, E., 2017. How business angel groups work: Rejection criteria in investment evaluation. *International Small Business Journal, 35*(4), pp. 405–426.

Cumming, D.J., Grilli, L. and Murtinu, S., 2017. Governmental and independent venture capital investments in Europe: A firm-level performance analysis. *Journal of Corporate Finance, 42*, pp. 439–459.

Cumming, D.J., Leboeuf, G. and Schwienbacher, A., 2015. Crowdfunding models: Keep-it-all vs. all-or-nothing. *Financial Management*, 1–30.

Dettwiler, P., Lindelöf, P. and Löfsten, H., 2006. Utility of location: A comparative survey between small new technology-based firms located on and off Science Parks – Implications for facilities management. *Technovation, 26*(4), pp. 506–517.

Di Pietro, F., Prencipe, A. and Majchrzak, A., 2018. Crowd equity investors: An underutilized asset for open innovation in startups. *California Management Review, 60*(2), pp. 43–70.

Di Pietro, F., Spagnoletti, P. and Prencipe, A., 2019. Fundraising across digital divide: Evidences from charity crowdfunding. In *Organizing for Digital Innovation* (pp. 111–124). Springer, Cham.

Dushnitsky, G., 2012. Corporate venture capital in the 21st century: An integral part of firms' innovation toolkit. In Cumming, D. (ed.), *Oxford Handbooks: The Oxford Handbook of Venture Capital* (pp. 156–210). Oxford University Press, New York.

Dushnitsky, G. and Lenox, M.J., 2006. When does corporate venture capital investment create firm value? *Journal of Business Venturing, 21*(6), pp. 753–772.

Dyer, J.H. and Singh, H., 1998. The relational view: Cooperative strategy and sources of interorganizational competitive advantage. *Academy of Management Review, 23*(4), pp. 660–679.

Ehrlich, S.B., De Noble, A.F., Moore, T. and Weaver, R.R., 1994. After the cash arrives: A comparative study of venture capital and private investor involvement in entrepreneurial firms. *Journal of Business Venturing, 9*(1), pp. 67–82.

Eisenmann, T.R., Parker, G. and Van Alstyne, M., 2009. Opening platforms: How, when and why? *Platforms, Markets and Innovation, 6*, pp. 131–162.

Freear, J., Sohl, J.E. and Wetzel Jr, W.E., 1995. Angels: Personal investors in the venture capital market. *Entrepreneurship & Regional Development*, 7(1), pp. 85–94.

Gaston, R.J., 1989. The scale of informal capital markets. *Small Business Economics, 1*(3), pp. 223–230.

Gerber, E.M., Hui, J.S. and Kuo, P.Y., 2012. Crowdfunding: Why people are motivated to post and fund projects on crowdfunding platforms. In *Proceedings of the International Workshop on Design, Influence, and Social Technologies: Techniques, Impacts and Ethics* (Vol. 2, No. 11, p. 10). Northwestern University, Evanston, IL.

Gilson, R.J., 2003. Engineering a venture capital market: Lessons from the American experience. *Stanford Law Review*, pp. 1067–1103.

Gorman, M. and Sahlman, W.A., 1989. What do venture capitalists do? *Journal of Business Venturing, 4*(4), pp. 231–248.

Grant, R.M. and Baden-Fuller, C., 2004. A knowledge accessing theory of strategic alliances. *Journal of Management Studies, 41*(1), pp. 61–84.

Haas, P., Blohm, I. and Leimeister, J.M., 2014. An empirical taxonomy of crowdfunding intermediaries. In *Proceedings of the Thirty Fifth International Conference on Information Systems* (ICIS 2014), Auckland, New Zealand.

Hackett, S.M. and Dilts, D.M., 2008. Inside the black box of business incubation: Study B – scale assessment, model refinement, and incubation outcomes. *The Journal of Technology Transfer, 33*(5), pp. 439–471.

Hagiu, A. and Wright, J., 2014. Marketplace or reseller? *Management Science, 61*(1), pp. 184–203.

Harms, M., 2007. What drives motivation to participate financially in a crowdfunding community? Master thesis, Vrije Universitaet Amsterdam.

Harrison, R.T., Mason, C.M. and Girling, P., 2004. Financial bootstrapping and venture development in the software industry. *Entrepreneurship & Regional Development, 16*(4), pp. 307–333.

Hellmann, T. and Puri, M., 2002. Venture capital and the professionalization of start-up firms: Empirical evidence. *The Journal of Finance, 57*(1), pp. 169–197.

Hill, S.A. and Birkinshaw, J., 2008. Strategy–organization configurations in corporate venture units: Impact on performance and survival. *Journal of Business Venturing, 23*(4), 423–444.

Hindle, K. and Lee, L., 2002. An exploratory investigation of informal venture capitalists in Singapore. *Venture Capital: An International Journal of Entrepreneurial Finance, 4*(2), pp. 169–177.

Hochberg, Y.V., 2016. Accelerating entrepreneurs and ecosystems: The seed accelerator model. *Innovation Policy and the Economy, 16*(1), pp. 25–51.

Hsu, D.H., 2004. What do entrepreneurs pay for venture capital affiliation? *The Journal of Finance, 59*(4), pp. 1805–1844.

Hsu, D.H., 2006. Venture capitalists and cooperative start-up commercialization strategy. *Management Science, 52*(2), pp. 204–219.

Hughes, M., Ireland, R.D. and Morgan, R.E., 2007. Stimulating dynamic value: Social capital and business incubation as a pathway to competitive success. *Long Range Planning, 40*(2), pp. 154–177.

Jackson III, W.E., Bates, T. and Bradford, W.D., 2012. Does venture capitalist activism improve investment performance? *Journal of Business Venturing, 27*(3), 342–354.

Jeng, L.A. and Wells, P.C., 2000. The determinants of venture capital funding: Evidence across countries. *Journal of Corporate Finance, 6*(3), pp. 241–289.

Jian, L. and Shin, J., 2015. Motivations behind donors' contributions to crowdfunded journalism. *Mass Communication and Society, 18*(2), pp. 165–185.

Kelly, P., 2007. Chapter 12 Business angel research: The road traveled and the journey ahead. In Landström H. (ed.), *Handbook of Research on Venture Capital* (Vol. 1, p. 315). Edward Elgar Publishing.

Kgoroeadira, R., Burke, A. and van Stel, A., 2019. Small business online loan crowdfunding: Who gets funded and what determines the rate of interest? *Small Business Economics, 52*(1), pp. 67–87.

Kirzner, I.M., 1973. *Competition and Entrepreneurship.* University of Chicago Press, Chicago, IL.

Kirzner, I.M., 1997. Entrepreneurial discovery and the competitive market process: An Austrian approach. *Journal of Economic Literature, 35*(1), pp. 60–85.

Kuppuswamy, V. and Bayus, B.L., 2017. Does my contribution to your crowdfunding project matter? *Journal of Business Venturing, 32*(1), pp. 72–89.

Lalkaka, R. and Bishop, J., 1996. *Business Incubators in Economic Development: An Initial Assessment in Industrializing Countries.* United Nations Development Programme, New York.

Leonard, D. and Swap, W., 2000. Gurus in the garage. *Harvard Business Review, 78*(6), pp. 71–78.

Löfsten, H. and Lindelöf, P., 2002. Science Parks and the growth of new technology-based firms – Academic-industry links, innovation and markets. *Research Policy, 31*(6), pp. 859–876.

Madill, J.J., Haines Jr, G.H. and RIding, A.L., 2005. The role of angels in technology SMEs: A link to venture capital. *Venture Capital*, 7(2), pp. 107–129.

Mason, C.M. and Harrison, R.T., 1996. Informal venture capital: A study of the investment process, the post-investment experience and investment performance. *Entrepreneurship & Regional Development, 8*(2), pp. 105–126.

Mason, C.M. and Harrison, R.T., 2002. Is it worth it? The rates of return from informal venture capital investments. *Journal of Business Venturing, 17*(3), pp. 211–236.

Matlay, H. and Sørheim, R., 2005. Business angels as facilitators for further finance: An exploratory study. *Journal of Small Business and Enterprise Development, 12*, pp. 178–191.

Mian, S.A., 1997. Assessing and managing the university technology business incubator: An integrative framework. *Journal of Business Venturing, 12*(4), pp. 251–285.

Mollick, E., 2014. The dynamics of crowdfunding: An exploratory study. *Journal of Business Venturing, 29*(1), pp. 1–16.

Mollick, E.R. and Kuppuswamy, V., 2014. After the campaign: Outcomes of crowdfunding. UNC Kenan-Flagler Research Paper, 2376997.

Morduch, J., 1999. The microfinance promise. *Journal of Economic Literature, 37*(4), pp. 1569–1614.

Paschen, J., 2017. Choose wisely: Crowdfunding through the stages of the startup life cycle. *Business Horizons, 60*(2), pp. 179–188.

Pauwels, C., Clarysse, B., Wright, M. and Van Hove, J., 2016. Understanding a new generation incubation model: The accelerator. *Technovation, 50*, pp. 13–24.

Penrose, E., 1959. *The Theory of the Growth of the Firm*. Oxford University Press, New York.

Sapienza, H.J., Manigart, S. and Vermeir, W., 1996. Venture capitalist governance and value added in four countries. *Journal of Business Venturing, 11*(6), pp. 439–469.

Schumpeter, J.A., 1947. The creative response in economic history. *The Journal of Economic History*, 7(2), pp. 149–159.

Schwartz, M., 2009. Beyond incubation: An analysis of firm survival and exit dynamics in the post-graduation period. *The Journal of Technology Transfer, 34*(4), pp. 403–421.

Schwartz, M., 2013. A control group study of incubators' impact to promote firm survival. *The Journal of Technology Transfer, 38*(3), pp. 302–331.

Schwienbacher, A. and Larralde, B., 2010. Crowdfunding of small entrepreneurial ventures. In *Handbook of Entrepreneurial Finance*. Oxford University Press, Oxford.

Soetanto, D.P. and Jack, S.L., 2013. Business incubators and the networks of technology-based firms. *The Journal of Technology Transfer, 38*(4), pp. 432–453.

Souitaris, V. and Zerbinati, S., 2014. How do corporate venture capitalists do deals? An exploration of corporate investment practices. *Strategic Entrepreneurship Journal, 8*(4), pp. 321–348.

Stinchcombe, A.L., 1965. Organizations and social structure. *Handbook of Organizations, 44*(2), pp. 142–193.

Stuart, T.E., Hoang, H. and Hybels, R.C., 1999. Interorganizational endorsements and the performance of entrepreneurial ventures. *Administrative Science Quarterly, 44*(2), pp. 315–349.

Tötterman, H. and Sten, J., 2005. Start-ups: Business incubation and social capital. *International Small Business Journal, 23*(5), pp. 487–511.

West III, G.P. and Noel, T.W., 2009. The impact of knowledge resources on new venture performance. *Journal of Small Business Management, 47*(1), pp. 1–22.

Wright, M., Westhead, P. and Sohl, J., 1998. Editors' introduction: Habitual entrepreneurs and angel investors. *Entrepreneurship Theory and Practice, 22*(4), pp. 5–22.

Yli-Renko, H., Autio, E. and Sapienza, H.J., 2001. Social capital, knowledge acquisition, and knowledge exploitation in young technology-based firms. *Strategic Management Journal*, *22*(6–7), pp. 587–613.

Zider, B., 1998. How venture capital works. *Harvard Business Review*, *76*(6), pp. 131–139.

Ziegler, T., Shneor, R., Garvey, K., Wenzlaff, K., Yerolemou, N., Hao, R. and Zhang, B., 2018. Expanding Horizons. *The 3rd European Alternative Finance Industry Report*. University of Cambridge, Cambridge Centre for Alternative Finance.

Ziegler, T., Shneor, R., Wenzlaff, K., Odorović, A., Johanson, D., Hao, R. and Ryll, L., 2019. *4th European Alternative Finance Benchmarking Report*. University of Cambridge, Cambridge Centre for Alternative Finance.

3

PREPARING FOR A SUCCESSFUL FUNDRAISING

This chapter provides an up-to-date review of studies investigating the factors associated with a successful crowdfunding campaign. We distinguish among individual, project, and contextual-level characteristics of a crowdfunding campaign that influence backers' or investors' decisions to support a project, thereby, influencing a company's fundraising success.

3.1 Creating a successful crowdfunding campaign

Although crowdfunding is a relatively new method of funding for start-ups and small ventures, it is becoming an increasingly relevant alternative financing means and is attracting a great deal of research attention. Worldwide, scholars are investigating this phenomenon in an attempt to propose a theoretical model able to explain the dynamics underlying crowdfunding and focusing, specifically, on two aspects: (1) the incentives and disincentives for embarking on or taking part in a crowdfunding project (see, e.g. Gerber et al., 2012; Allison et al., 2015; Walthoff-Borm et al., 2018); and (2) the factors associated with a successful campaign (see, e.g. Agrawal et al., 2015; Mollick, 2014; Colombo et al., 2015; Giudici et al., 2018; Butticè et al., 2017).

In Section 2.2, we discussed what drives entrepreneurs to use crowdfunding. We referred, specifically, to the fact that fundraisers see crowdfunding as an opportunity to obtain financing for their companies at lower capital cost, to attract public attention, and to obtain feedback on the product or service on offer (Gerber et al., 2012; Agrawal et al., 2015; Belleflamme et al., 2014; Mollick, 2014). The benefits derived by crowd funders keen to support an innovative idea include early access to new products and belonging to a community (of crowd funders) (Zhang, 2012; Agrawal et al., 2015).

In Chapter 3, we distinguish among project-level, individual-level, and contextual-level characteristics and explore the different aspects affecting crowdfunding project success. Table 3.1 illustrates factors considered predictors of crowdfunding campaign success.

TABLE 3.1 Projects, individual, and contextual-level predictors of crowdfunding success

Authors	*Type of crowdfunding*	*Factors*	*Influence on campaign success*
Crowdfunding project characteristics			
Ahlerset al. (2015)	Equity crowdfunding	Project risk	Positive
		Founding team experience	Positive
Allison et al. (2015)	Lending crowdfunding	Positive, pro-social language	Positive
Bernstein et al. (2017)	Equity and reward crowdfunding	Information on founding team	Positive
		Entrepreneur human capital	Positive
Davis et al. (2017)	Reward crowdfunding	Entrepreneur passion and product originality	Positive
Di Pietro and Masciarelli (2019)	Equity crowdfunding	Company past achievements and milestones	Positive
Frydrych et al. (2014)	Reward crowdfunding	Campaign duration	Negative
		Solo entrepreneurs	Negative
		Team of co-founders	Positive
Gorbatai and Nelson (2015)	Reward crowdfunding	Positive and inclusive language	Positive
		Business language	Negative
Kim and Viswanathan (2019)	Reward crowdfunding	Participation of expert investors (e.g.VCs)	Positive
Mollick (2014)	Reward crowdfunding	Campaign duration	Negative
		Target amount	Negative
Parhankangas and Renko (2017)	Reward crowdfunding	Concrete language	Positive
Steigenberger and Wilhelm (2018)	Reward crowdfunding	Rhetorical signals	Positive
Entrepreneur characteristics			
Agrawal et al. (2011)	Reward crowdfunding	Family and friends	Positive
Butticè et al. (2017)	Reward crowdfunding	Entrepreneur internal social capital	Positive
		Entrepreneur prior crowdfunding experience	Positive

(*Continued*)

TABLE 3.1 (Continued)

Authors	*Type of crowdfunding*	*Factors*	*Influence on campaign success*
Colombo et al. (2015)	Reward crowdfunding	Entrepreneur internal social capital	Positive
		Early backers	Positive
Courtney et al. (2017)	Reward crowdfunding	Entrepreneur prior crowdfunding experience Third-party endorsement	Positive
		Use of social media	
Kgoroeadira et al. (2019)	Lending crowdfunding	Entrepreneur personal characteristics (e.g. credit profile, borrowing history)	Positive
Lin et al. (2013)	Lending crowdfunding	Borrower network	Positive
Piva and Rossi-Lamastra (2018)	Equity crowdfunding	Entrepreneur human capital	Positive
Vismara (2016)	Equity crowdfunding	Entrepreneur social capital	Positive
Vismara (2018)	Equity crowdfunding	Information sharing, Investors public profile	Positive
Contextual characteristics			
Agrawal et al. (2015)	Reward crowdfunding	Geographic proximity	Positive
Di Pietro et al. (2019)	Donation crowdfunding	Digital literacy	Positive
		Digital divide	Negative
Giudici et al. (2018)	Reward crowdfunding	Local altruism	Positive
Guenther et al. (2018)	Equity crowdfunding	Geographic distance	Negative
Lin and Viswanathan (2015)	Lending crowdfunding	Geographic proximity	Positive
Mollick (2014)	Reward crowdfunding	Geographic proximity	Positive
Ordanini et al. (2011)	Reward crowdfunding	Geographic proximity	Positive

3.1.1 Crowdfunding project characteristics

One of most important factors affecting fundraising success is campaign duration (Mollick, 2014). Most platforms require the entrepreneur to define a campaign duration of between 30 and 60 days, although some platforms allow fundraising campaigns to remain live for up to 90 days. Research shows that shorter campaigns, less than 30 days on average, have a higher chance of success. This is because a longer campaign can be discouraging to investors who might perceive an extended period for fundraising as a sign of the entrepreneur's lack of confidence in eventual success (Mollick, 2014; Frydrych et al., 2014).

It is important that prospective backers are provided with extensive and detailed information on the proposed company, to reduce information asymmetries and increase commitment (Ahlers et al., 2015; Vismara, 2018; Hoenig and Henkel, 2015). Entrepreneurial ventures, inevitably, lack a track record and, especially in the case of innovative high-tech ventures, often have high levels of intangible assets (Walthoff-Borm et al., 2018). It is also inevitable that the entrepreneur will be optimistic about the chances of success and may be tempted to misrepresent the business (Shane and Cable, 2002; Shane and Stuart, 2002). In the absence of standard means of evaluation, it is difficult for potential funders to evaluate the proposed company's quality and identify "signals" or "certification" of good quality (Dewally and Ederington, 2006; Kuppuswammy and Roth, 2016). Therefore providing detailed information about the project and the founding team (Ahlers et al., 2015; Bernstein et al., 2017), and being able to provide certification from stakeholders (Bapna, 2017; Ahlers et al., 2015) and expert investors (Kim and Viswanathan, 2019), are all ways of increasing the trustworthiness of the campaign.

However, an often overlooked aspect is the importance of having a team of people with distinctive roles and specific individual responsibilities. It seems that, understandably, crowdfunding campaigns involving companies with at least two co-founders or a co-founding team, achieve much higher success rates than projects headed by an individual entrepreneur (Frydrych et al., 2014).

Research that examines in more depth how entrepreneurs design their campaigns shows that storytelling is a powerful means for establishing venture legitimacy and gaining crowd support. Research focusing on the linguistic features of crowdfunding campaign suggests that campaigns couched in positive, vivid, and inclusive language are more likely to be successful than campaign that use business jargon (Gorbatai and Nelson, 2015; Allison et al., 2015). It has been shown that use of clear and precise language, and adoption of an interactive style, are fundamental for social crowdfunding campaign success (Parhankangas and Renko, 2017). Also, rhetoric signals (Steigenberger and Wilhelm, 2018), demonstration of entrepreneurial passion, as well as the originality of the product, increase the entrepreneur's ability to collect funding (Davis et al., 2017).

Entrepreneurs can increase their fundraising success rate via the crowd by providing detailed information on their companies' past achievements and future plans (Di Pietro and Masciarelli, 2019). Common themes related to company's past achievements are previous fundraising activity, for example, whether the company had received some funding before the crowdfunding campaign; clients' or users' acquisition; recognition from external parties, for instance media coverage, company awards, partnerships, and collaborations. In relation to development plans, entrepreneurs inform the crowd about product development activities, company expansion strategy, in the local market or in a foreign country, as well as their intention to participate to fairs and other industry events.

3.1.2 Entrepreneur characteristics

Entrepreneurs' social capital is one of the most important factors influencing crowdfunding campaign success (see, e.g. Colombo et al., 2015; Butticè et al., 2017; Vismara, 2016). The relationships and social contacts involving founders and potential backers on the online platform – defined as internal social capital – appear to be fundamental for influencing the chances that investors will contribute to the project (Colombo et al., 2015). A history of previous successful campaigns is one way that project proponents can build internal social capital and increase the chances of the current campaign being successful (Butticè et al., 2017; Courtney et al., 2017). Chapter 2 showed that family and friends are relevant to crowdfunding investment: the entrepreneur's friends and family network are an important resource for campaign success since they tend to invest early in the funding cycle, which signals the quality of the business to subsequent investors (Mollick, 2014; Agrawal et al., 2011; Colombo et al., 2015). Also, several studies show that early backers play a critical role in attracting subsequent investments through a signalling mechanism which demonstrates project quality (Colombo et al., 2015; Ahlers et al., 2015). Vismara (2018) confirmed the importance of information sharing, suggesting that investors with a public profile increase the appeal of the offer among early investors, who in turn attract late investors.

Another factor influencing fundraising success is the entrepreneur's human capital, such as skills, knowledge, and experienced possessed. For instance, among other characteristics, entrepreneur's education and previous business, and industry experience have been shown to be relevant for attracting higher numbers of investors (e.g. Piva and Rossi-Lamastra, 2018; Bernstein et al., 2017).

Essentially, crowdfunding depends on attracting a crowd; therefore, entrepreneurs need to exploit their networks to obtain support and achieve campaign success (Vismara, 2016). The power of social media has been shown to be critical in the crowdfunding context. Entrepreneurs with large personal social networks (Mollick, 2014), who are active on social media, and demonstrate an understanding of social media selectivity, that is the use different social media depending on their target audience, are more likely to result in a successful crowdfunding campaign outcome (Nevin et al., 2017; Courtney et al., 2017).

3.1.3 Contextual factors

There is an important stream of literature that focuses on the effect of contextual factors on crowdfunding campaign success. Although the Internet facilitates world-wide connections and reduces distance-related frictions, geographic distance has been shown to be an impediment to crowdfunding. Research shows that transactions are more likely between entrepreneurs and backers residing in the same geographical area (Ordanini et al., 2011; Mollick, 2014; Guenther et al., 2018) and that the early contributors to crowdfunding projects are more likely to be local investors (Agrawal et al., 2011, 2015). Therefore, despite the availability of technology, in the case of financial products, there is a persisting home bias in this virtual marketplace (Lin and Viswanathan, 2015; Hortaçsu et al., 2009).

In addition to physical distance, the characteristics of the local area of the project proponent have an influence on fundraising success. For instance, local altruism (Giudici et al., 2018), that is, the level of altruism among the people living in the same city as the project proponent, and local religiosity (Di Pietro et al., 2018) has been shown to be important for crowdfunding project success.

Other contextual factors influencing crowdfunding are related to the availability of a communication infrastructure to support crowdfunding interactions, and the e-skills and capabilities of the people involved in the business. For instance, e-payment systems, such as mobile banking, can be used to transfer the investments to the recipient. However, access to these tools is restricted to users with a connection to the Internet and the ability to perform online transactions. In this context, research shows that a low level of digital divide, that is, the possibility to access infrastructure such as broadband connection, and a high level of digital literacy, that is, habitual use of the Internet, enhance the propensity for potential investors to invest using a crowdfunding platform (Di Pietro et al., 2019).

References

Agrawal, A., Catalini, C. and Goldfarb, A., 2015. Crowdfunding: Geography, social networks, and the timing of investment decisions. *Journal of Economics & Management Strategy*, *24*(2), pp. 253–274.

Agrawal, A.K., Catalini, C. and Goldfarb, A., 2011. *The Geography of Crowdfunding* (No. w16820). National Bureau of Economic Research, Cambridge, MA.

Ahlers, G.K., Cumming, D., Günther, C. and Schweizer, D., 2015. Signaling in equity crowdfunding. *Entrepreneurship Theory and Practice*, *39*(4), pp. 955–980.

Allison, T.H., Davis, B.C., Short, J.C. and Webb, J.W., 2015. Crowdfunding in a prosocial microlending environment: Examining the role of intrinsic versus extrinsic cues. *Entrepreneurship Theory and Practice*, *39*(1), pp. 53–73.

Bapna, S., 2017. Complementarity of signals in early-stage equity investment decisions: Evidence from a randomized field experiment. *Management Science*, *65*(2), pp. 933–952.

Belleflamme, P., Lambert, T. and Schwienbacher, A., 2014. Crowdfunding: Tapping the right crowd. *Journal of Business Venturing*, *29*(5), pp. 585–609.

Bernstein, S., Korteweg, A. and Laws, K., 2017. Attracting early-stage investors: Evidence from a randomized field experiment. *The Journal of Finance*, *72*(2), pp. 509–538.

Butticè, V., Colombo, M.G. and Wright, M., 2017. Serial crowdfunding, social capital, and project success. *Entrepreneurship Theory and Practice*, *41*(2), pp. 183–207.

Colombo, M.G., Franzoni, C. and Rossi–Lamastra, C., 2015. Internal social capital and the attraction of early contributions in crowdfunding. *Entrepreneurship Theory and Practice*, *39*(1), pp. 75–100.

Courtney, C., Dutta, S. and Li, Y., 2017. Resolving information asymmetry: Signaling, endorsement, and crowdfunding success. *Entrepreneurship Theory and Practice, 41*(2), pp. 265–290.

Davis, B.C., Hmieleski, K.M., Webb, J.W. and Coombs, J.E., 2017. Funders' positive affective reactions to entrepreneurs' crowdfunding pitches: The influence of perceived product creativity and entrepreneurial passion. *Journal of Business Venturing, 32*(1), pp. 90–106.

Dewally, M. and Ederington, L., 2006. Reputation, certification, warranties, and information as remedies for seller-buyer information asymmetries: Lessons from the online comic book market. *The Journal of Business, 79*(2), pp. 693–729.

Di Pietro, F. and Masciarelli, F., 2019. What the crowd values the most in financing innovative campaigns? The role of future vs. past oriented signals. *4th Entrepreneurial Finance Conference*, Trier, Germany.

Di Pietro, F., Masciarelli, F. and Prencipe A., 2018. Believe or not believe? The effect of religiosity on individuals' participation on reward-based crowdfunding projects. In Colombo, M.G., Giudici, G. (eds.), *3rd Entrepreneurial Finance Conference*, Milan, Politecnico di Milano, School of Management.

Di Pietro, F., Spagnoletti, P. and Prencipe, A., 2019. Fundraising across digital divide: Evidences from charity crowdfunding. In *Organizing for Digital Innovation* (pp. 111–124). Springer, Cham.

Frydrych, D., Bock, A.J., Kinder, T. and Koeck, B., 2014. Exploring entrepreneurial legitimacy in reward-based crowdfunding. *Venture Capital, 16*(3), pp. 247–269.

Gerber, E.M., Hui, J.S. and Kuo, P.Y., 2012. February. Crowdfunding: Why people are motivated to post and fund projects on crowdfunding platforms. In *Proceedings of the International Workshop on Design, Influence, and Social Technologies: Techniques, Impacts and Ethics* (Vol. 2, No. 11, p. 10). Northwestern University, Evanston, IL.

Giudici, G., Guerini, M. and Rossi-Lamastra, C., 2018. Reward-based crowdfunding of entrepreneurial projects: The effect of local altruism and localized social capital on proponents' success. *Small Business Economics, 50*(2), pp. 307–324.

Gorbatai, A.D. and Nelson, L., 2015. Gender and the language of crowdfunding. In *Academy of Management Proceedings* (Vol. 2015, No. 1, p. 15785). Academy of Management, Briarcliff Manor, NY.

Guenther, C., Johan, S. and Schweizer, D., 2018. Is the crowd sensitive to distance? – How investment decisions differ by investor type. *Small Business Economics, 50*(2), pp. 289–305.

Hoenig, D. and Henkel, J., 2015. Quality signals? The role of patents, alliances, and team experience in venture capital financing. *Research Policy, 44*(5), pp. 1049–1064.

Hortaçsu, A., Martínez-Jerez, F. and Douglas, J., 2009. The geography of trade in online transactions: Evidence from eBay and mercadolibre. *American Economic Journal: Microeconomics, 1*(1), pp. 53–74.

Kgoroeadira, R., Burke, A. and van Stel, A., 2019. Small business online loan crowdfunding: Who gets funded and what determines the rate of interest? *Small Business Economics, 52*(1), pp. 67–87.

Kim, K. and Viswanathan, S., 2019. The experts in the crowd: The role of experienced investors in a crowdfunding market. *MIS Quarterly, 43*(2), pp. 347–372.

Kuppuswammy, V. and Roth, K., 2016. Research on the current state of crowdfunding: The effect of crowdfunding performance and outside capital. *US Small Business Administration-Office of Advocacy.*

Lin, M., Prabhala, N.R. and Viswanathan, S., 2013. Judging borrowers by the company they keep: Friendship networks and information asymmetry in online peer-to-peer lending. *Management Science, 59*(1), pp. 17–35.

Lin, M. and Viswanathan, S., 2015. Home bias in online investments: An empirical study of an online crowdfunding market. *Management Science, 62*(5), pp. 1393–1414.
Mollick, E., 2014. The dynamics of crowdfunding: An exploratory study. *Journal of Business Venturing, 29*(1), pp. 1–16.
Nevin, S., Gleasure, R., O'Reilly, P., Feller, J., Li, S. and Cristoforo, J., 2017, August. Social identity and social media activities in equity crowdfunding. In *Proceedings of the 13th International Symposium on Open Collaboration* (p. 11). ACM, New York, NY.
Ordanini, A., Miceli, L., Pizzetti, M. and Parasuraman, A., 2011. Crowd-funding: Transforming customers into investors through innovative service platforms. *Journal of Service Management, 22*(4), pp. 443–470.
Parhankangas, A. and Renko, M., 2017. Linguistic style and crowdfunding success among social and commercial entrepreneurs. *Journal of Business Venturing, 32*(2), pp. 215–236.
Piva, E. and Rossi-Lamastra, C., 2018. Human capital signals and entrepreneurs' success in equity crowdfunding. *Small Business Economics, 51*(3), pp. 667–686.
Shane, S. and Cable, D., 2002. Network ties, reputation, and the financing of new ventures. *Management Science, 48*(3), pp. 364–381.
Shane, S. and Stuart, T., 2002. Organizational endowments and the performance of university start-ups. *Management Science, 48*(1), pp. 154–170.
Steigenberger, N. and Wilhelm, H., 2018. Extending signaling theory to rhetorical signals: Evidence from crowdfunding. *Organization Science, 29*(3), pp. 529–546.
Vismara, S., 2016. Equity retention and social network theory in equity crowdfunding. *Small Business Economics, 46*(4), pp. 579–590.
Vismara, S., 2018. Information cascades among investors in equity crowdfunding. *Entrepreneurship Theory and Practice, 42*(3), pp. 467–497.
Walthoff-Borm, X., Schwienbacher, A. and Vanacker, T., 2018. Equity crowdfunding: First resort or last resort? *Journal of Business Venturing, 33*(4), pp. 513–533.
Zhang, Y., 2012. An empirical study into the field of crowdfunding, Master thesis dissertation, Lund University. Available at http://lup.lub.lu.se/luur/download?func=downloadFile&recordOId=3049774&fileOId=3049777

4

THE GEOGRAPHY OF CROWDFUNDING

Crowdfunding is an important financing tool for new businesses and a source of national economic and technological development. However, some countries benefit more than others from crowdfunding. This variation in levels of crowdfunding across countries reflects their stage of economic development, which, often, is linked to their location, institutional characteristics, and informal cultural constraints. In Chapter 4, we explore differences in the adoption of crowdfunding across the globe, considering the three macro regions of Europe, America, and Asia Pacific, and examine the role of formal and informal institutional development in influencing the adoption of crowdfunding.

4.1 Crowdfunding across countries: an overview

Since its inception, the crowdfunding markets in Europe and the rest of the world have experienced exponential regional- and country-level growth. In the United States, one of the world's largest and most innovative countries for alternative financing, the total amount raised via crowdfunding in 2017 was US$42 billion (Ziegler et al., 2018a). Another important area, in terms of development of the crowdfunding market, is the Asia Pacific region, whose main regional markets include China, Oceania, and South Asia. China is the market leader, accounting for 99.2% of total Asia Pacific crowdfunding market (Ziegler et al., 2018b). In 2017, total transactions in China amounted to US$358 billion, representing annual growth of 46% compared to 2016.

Figure 4.1 presents total transaction amounts in 2017 in three main market: Europe, US, and China. It shows that in 2017, China was the biggest market in terms of funds raised by companies via crowdfunding, followed by the US and then Europe, with a total amount of US$10 billion.

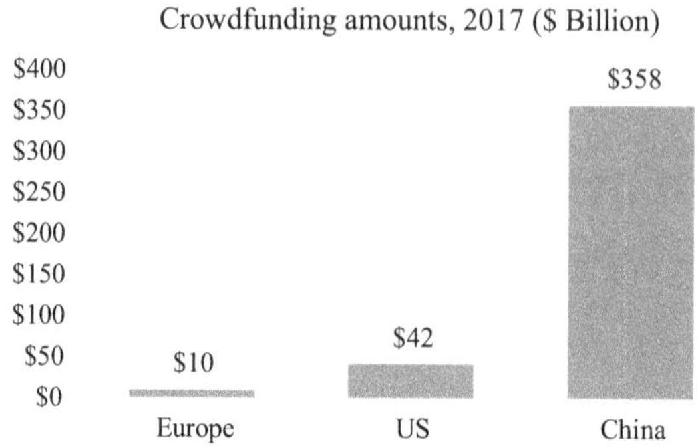

FIGURE 4.1 Crowdfunding amounts: Europe, US, and China, 2017

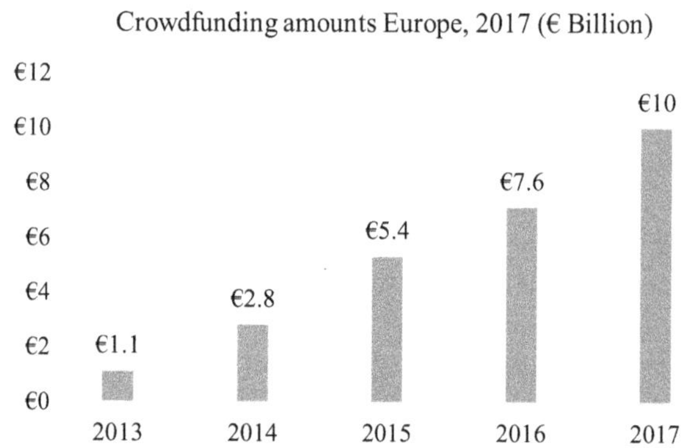

FIGURE 4.2 Crowdfunding amounts: Europe, 2013–2017

In Europe, the overall market increased by 41% annually, from €5.4 billion in 2015 to €7.6 billion in 2016, and grew by 36% in 2017 to reach €10 billion (Ziegler et al., 2019) (see Figure 4.2). Between 2013 and 2017, the average annual rate of growth of crowdfunding in Europe was 80%.

This growth was driven by a dramatic increase in the UK market (accounting for 70% of the entire European market in 2017) and the rapid expansion of alternative finance markets in some of the smaller European countries such as the Nordic countries, the Iberian Peninsula, and the Baltic states. France is ranked second after the UK for transaction amounts and accounted for 7% of the European crowdfunding market in 2017, with €661 million raised via crowdfunding platforms. Germany and the Netherlands markets are ranked third and fourth, respectively, together account for 9% of the total European crowdfunding market (see Figure 4.3).

All crowdfunding models have experienced dramatic growth in Europe, although during the last year considered (2017), this growth declined somewhat.

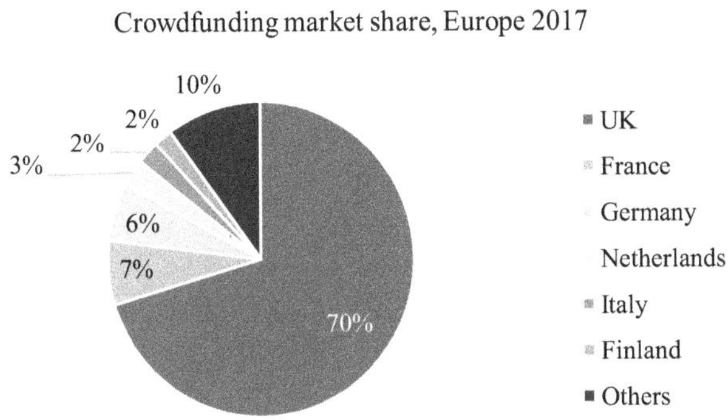

FIGURE 4.3 Crowdfunding market share: Europe, 2017

Lending crowdfunding is the most popular crowdfunding investment model in Europe (Ziegler et al., 2019). Peer-to-peer (P2P) consumer and business lending accounted for about 51% of the total crowdfunding market in 2017 (see Figure 4.4). Equity-based and reward-based crowdfunding declined in 2017, with each accounting for approximately 10% of the market. Donation-based platforms saw modest growth in 2017, but account for only 1.6% of the market.

P2P lending is the dominant crowdfunding model, also, in the US and accounted for 61% of the market in 2017, followed by the equity-based model (Ziegler et al., 2018a). P2P lending is the main model in Asia, and accounted for 56% of the total China and Australian markets and 60% of the total Asian market (Ziegler et al., 2018b).

Figure 4.4 depicts the most popular crowdfunding models. Lending crowdfunding is the most frequent in all three macro regions. Equity crowdfunding represents 15% of market transactions, on average. The remaining crowdfunding categories, such as donation-based and reward-based crowdfunding, as well as other forms of alternative finance, that is, mini bonds, P2P property lending, invoice trading, real estate crowdfunding, etc., account for an important proportion, averaging 30% of the overall crowdfunding market.

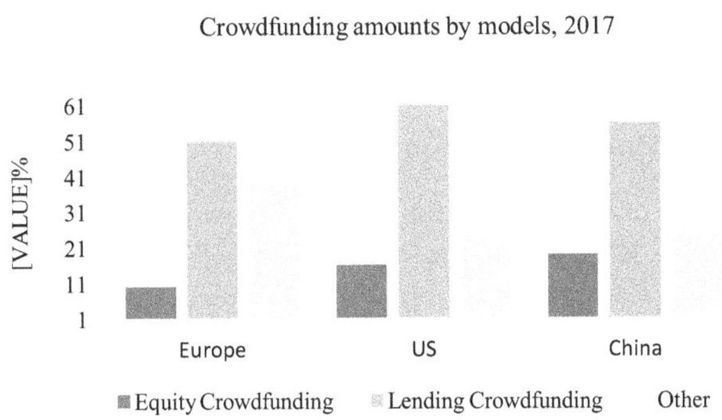

FIGURE 4.4 Crowdfunding amounts by models: Europe, US, and China, 2017

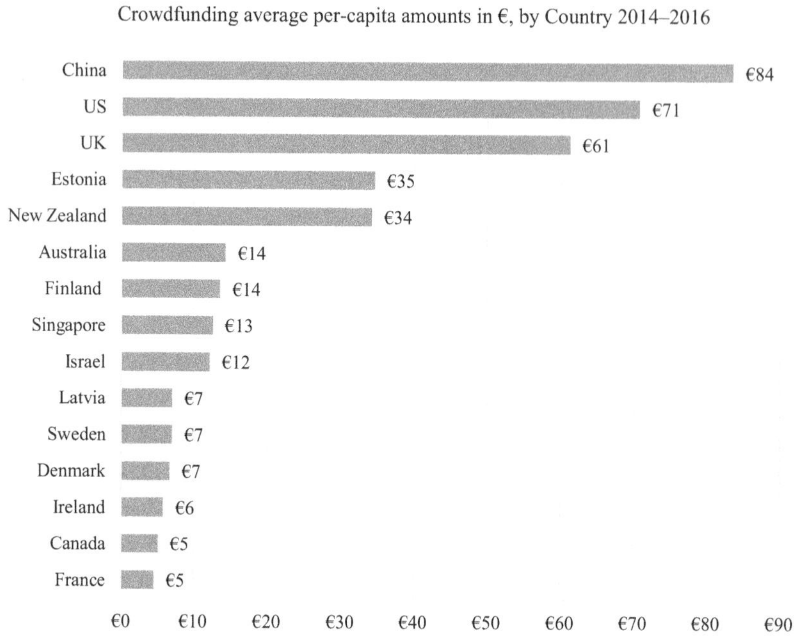

FIGURE 4.5 Crowdfunding average per capita amounts by country, 2014–2016

To allow a more accurate assessment of countries' propensity to use crowdfunding, we classify countries based on the per capita amount invested by their populations. Figure 4.5 is a bar chart showing the average per capita amount invested in different countries, between 2014 and 2016, based on all crowdfunding forms.

China and the US are the most active countries. Between 2014 and 2016, Chinese and Americans invested, respectively, €84 and €71 per capita, in different types of crowdfunding. In Europe, the UK is the most active investor in alternative financing, registering an average of €61 per capita investment, although Estonia and Finland, which are small countries, have a higher propensity for crowdfunding investment than France and Germany, which are the second and third largest European markets in terms of total transaction amounts (see Figure 4.3).

4.2 Crowdfunding in Europe: the main players

Chapter 3 showed that the European market for crowdfunding, although smaller than the Asian and US markets, has shown continued growth and reached more than €10 billion of transactions (see Figure 4.6). The UK is the leader for adoption of crowdfunding as a financing tool, followed by France and Germany. The crowdfunding activity has been slower in the Benelux countries (Netherlands, Belgium, and Luxembourg), the Nordic countries (Denmark, Sweden, Norway, Iceland, and Finland) and Italy, but is increasing (Ziegler et al., 2019).

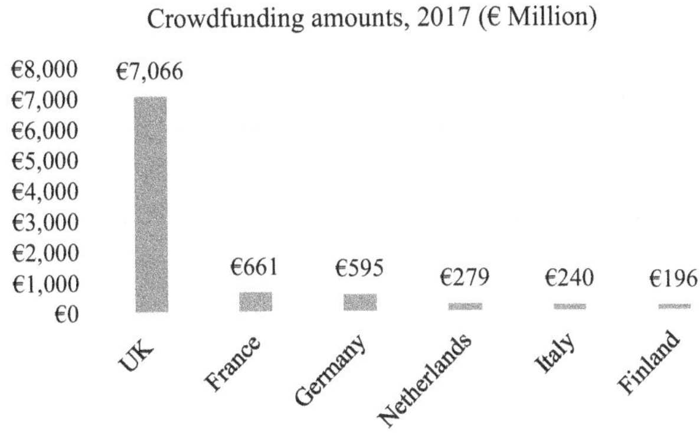

FIGURE 4.6 Crowdfunding amounts: main European countries, 2017

An important factor that is promoting the continuous development of crowdfunding is the adoption of a specific legal framework at the European and country level. This is especially important in relation to equity crowdfunding, which allows non-professional investors to acquire shares in non-listed companies (see Section 5.1 for more detail) and requires regulatory intervention to protect small investors from potential fraud risks. To create a single capital market, the European Union (EU), in March 2018, introduced the Regulation on European Crowdfunding Service Providers (ECSP),[1] which proposes a voluntary EU regime for lending-based and equity-based crowdfunding service providers (i.e. platforms). The aim of this regulation is to provide a "minimum harmonisation" of regulation of crowdfunding across Europe, to protect investors and platforms, increase use of this tool, and enable cross country transactions. However, due to differences in the regulation across European countries, crowdfunding remains a local phenomenon, and cross-border transactions represent only a small proportion, about 10%, of overall transactions (Ziegler et al., 2019). Although the European voluntary regulation is in place, it does not replace national regulation.

In what follows, we undertake a deeper investigation of the crowdfunding phenomenon in the main European crowdfunding markets, in terms of transaction amounts. The countries examined are the UK, as market leader, and France, Germany, and the Netherlands, which are the top three countries measured by transaction amounts, and account for about 50% of the European region's investment amounts (excluding the UK).

4.2.1 The UK

The UK crowdfunding market in 2017 accounted for 71% (or 7.1 billion euro of transactions) of the total European market. Between 2012 and 2017, UK companies raised around €20 billion. For seven consecutive years, the UK crowdfunding market has grown, reaching a peak in 2013 and 2014 (see Figure 4.7).

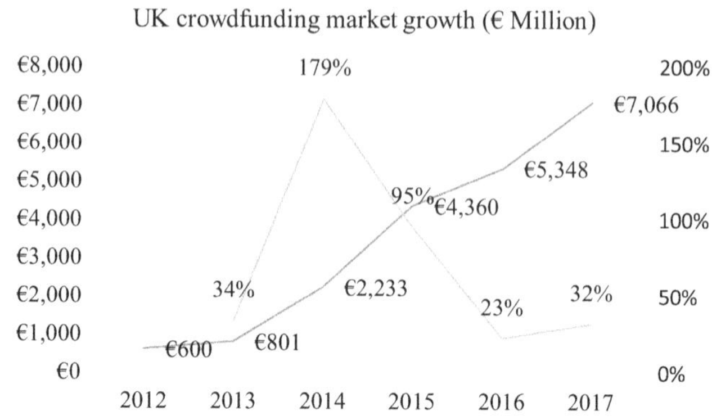

FIGURE 4.7 Crowdfunding market growth: UK, 2012–2017

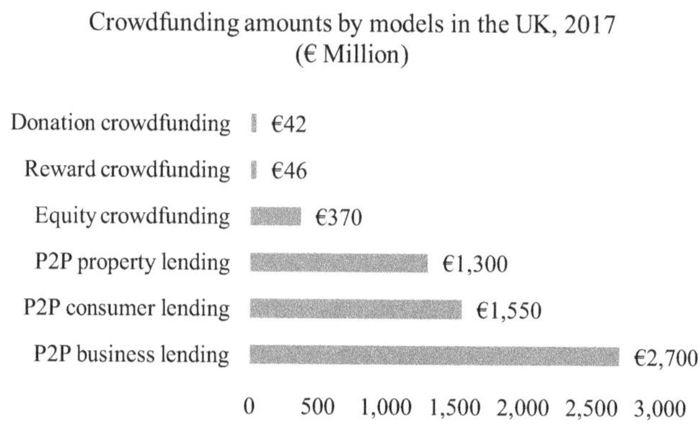

FIGURE 4.8 Crowdfunding amounts by models: UK, 2017

The most frequent crowdfunding model is lending crowdfunding. P2P business lending refers to loans provided to business borrowers by individuals or institutional funders and is the most popular alternative finance model worth €2.7 billion in 2017. P2P consumer lending, which includes loans provided to consumer borrowers, was worth €1.55 billion (see Figure 4.8).

Transactions amounts raised on equity-based crowdfunding platforms in UK in 2017 reached €370 million, an increase of 22% compared to 2016. Other models, such as reward-based and donation-based crowdfunding, reached about €90 million, similar to the amount raised in 2016.

In terms of the number of companies that fundraised via crowdfunding, in 2017 approximately 29,000 firms chose this alternative financing model, a slight decrease on the 33,000 companies financed in 2016.

In the UK, Funding Circle and LendInvest are the biggest P2P lending platform; the two main equity crowdfunding players are Seedrs and Crowdcube (see Chapter 5).

4.2.2 *France, Germany, and the Netherlands*

In 2017, France was ranked second after the UK for use of crowdfunding in Europe, and grew 40% compared to the 2016. In 2017, the French market accounted for 7% of total alternative finance amounts in Europe, reaching over €660 million. In Germany crowdfunding has grown steadily since 2012 (see Figure 4.9), increasing from €249 million in 2015 to €595 million in 2017. The Netherlands is the fourth biggest market in Europe, accounting for 79% of the amount invested in the Benelux region (Netherlands, Belgium, and Luxembourg). The market in Benelux grew by 67% in 2016, making it the fifth largest market for alternative finance with over of €350 million in 2017. In the Netherlands companies raise about €280 million through crowdfunding platforms in 2017, registering a massive growth – about 150% – compared to the amount transacted 2015.

The adoption of different crowdfunding models by these three countries reflects the trend in continental Europe. Figure 4.10 shows that in these three countries, P2P lending is the most frequent crowdfunding type, followed by equity-based and reward-based crowdfunding.

In Germany, there is huge debate about equity-based crowdfunding and, in 2017, Germany undertook a review of the crowdfunding regulation. Investor behaviour changed radically after several start-ups became insolvent in 2017. This has led to greater caution in Germany, about using equity crowdfunding as an alternative investment vehicle (Ziegler et al., 2019).

In 2016, the Netherlands introduced a specific regime for P2P lending and equity investment models to reduce uncertainty among investors and promote adoption of crowdfunding.

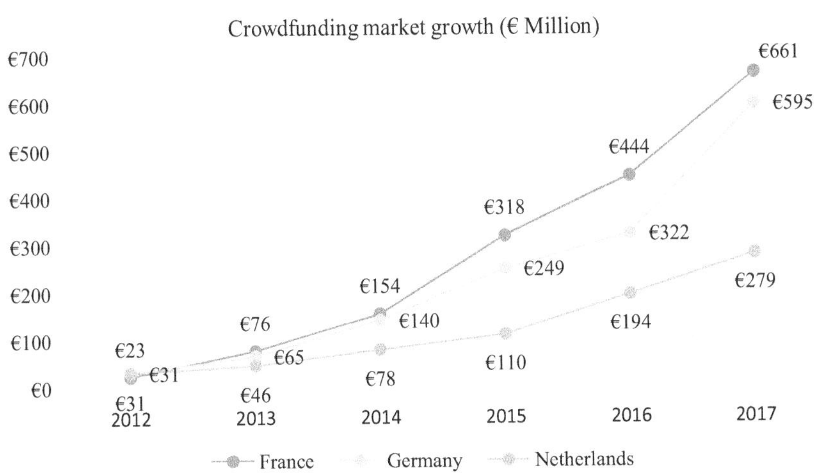

FIGURE 4.9 Crowdfunding market growth: France, Germany, and the Netherlands, 2012–2017

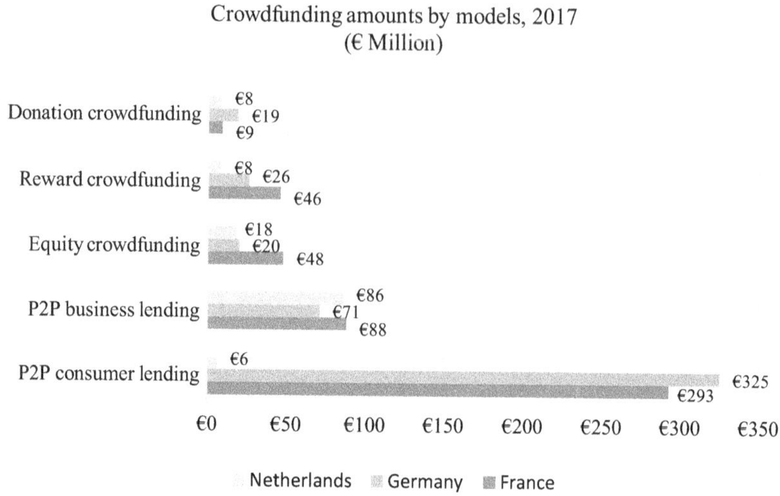

FIGURE 4.10 Crowdfunding amounts by models: France, Germany, and the Netherlands, 2017

The best-known equity crowdfunding platforms in France are Wiseed and Anaxago. Also, popular is, Prêt d'Union, a P2P consumer lending platform. The most important reward crowdfunding platforms are Kiss Kiss Bank Bank. In Germany, Seedmatch and Companisto are well known; they allow exchanges of equity for shares in private companies, while Betterplace, which is a donation-based crowdfunding platform, focuses on social projects. Auxoney is a P2P lending platform founded in 2007 in Germany, which has more than 4 million investors.

The most popular platforms in Netherlands are Symbid and GeldVoorElkaar. The first is an equity-based platform launched in 2011, which has funded more than 209 businesses, representing more than €29 million in funding from 53,000 registered members. GeldVoorElkaar is the largest P2P business lending platform established in 2010. It accounts for more than €155 million of transactions, related to around 1,400 businesses.

4.2.3 The rest of Europe

Although only few countries account for most of the European crowdfunding market (see Figure 4.3), the Nordic countries, including Finland and Sweden, and some Eastern European countries, such as Estonia, are performing well in terms of total transaction amounts (see Figure 4.11).

To compare European countries, we consider country size and average per capita amount invested. Figure 4.12 shows that inventors in some small countries, such as Finland and Estonia, are active in using crowdfunding platforms for investment purposes or obtaining support for creative and innovative projects.

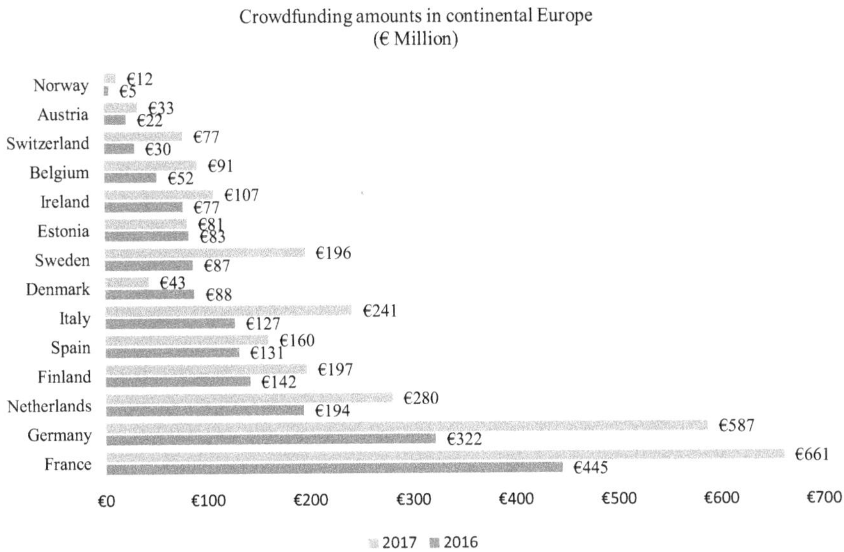

FIGURE 4.11 Crowdfunding volume in Europe by country, 2016–2017

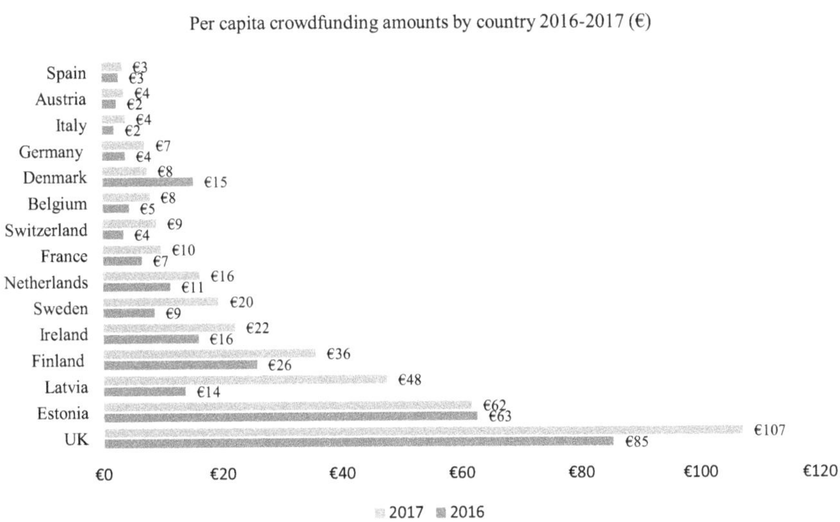

FIGURE 4.12 Per capita crowdfunding amounts in Europe by country, 2016–2017

Ireland and Sweden are also performing well, with average per capita investment of around €20 per year in 2017. Figure 4.12 also shows that the two biggest markets after the UK – France and Germany – are ranked lower measured by per capita amounts invested. These data reflect the differences in individual investment behaviour related to crowdfunding across Europe.

4.3 The American market

In 2017, the total value of the American market, which includes the US, Canada, and the Latin American countries[2] (LAC) was some US$44 billion, an increase of 26% on the US$32.5 billion invested in 2016. In the five years between 2013–2017, companies in the American region have raised over US$124 billion (of which 35% invested in 2017) to finance their development (Ziegler et al., 2018a). The US accounts for the majority of the American market share, representing 97% of transaction amounts in 2017. Canada follows with 2% of the crowdfunding market, with the remaining 1% represented by the LAC (see Figure 4.13).

In the US, in 2017, about US$43 billion were invested via different crowdfunding models. Since 2012, the US market has experienced relevant market growth, in 2017 reaching more than three times the transaction amount registered in 2014. Figure 4.14 illustrates the evolution of the crowdfunding market in the US.

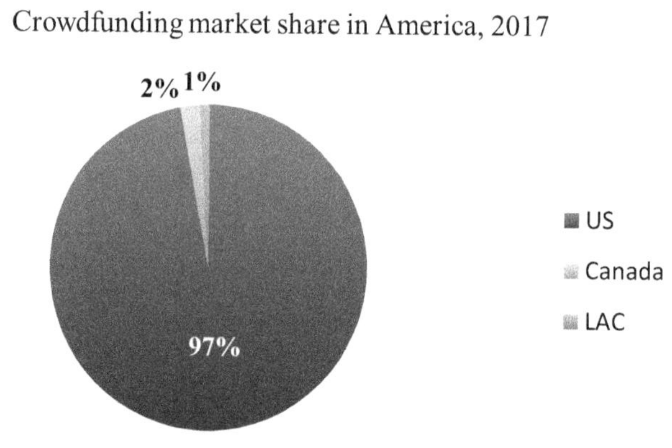

FIGURE 4.13 Crowdfunding market share: America, 2017

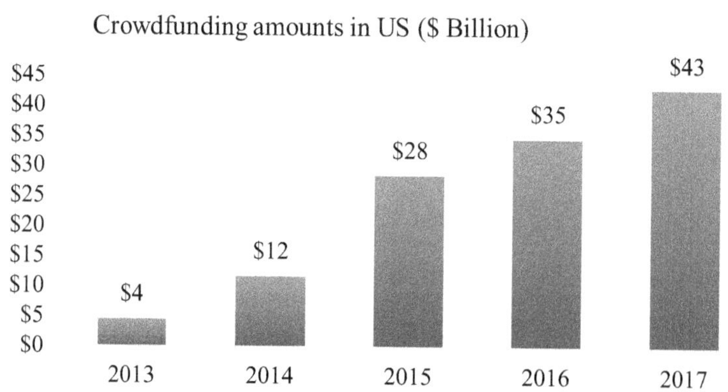

FIGURE 4.14 Crowdfunding investment amounts: US, 2013–2017

Canada, the second biggest market, reached US$868 million invested in crowdfunding in 2017, a growth of 170% compared to 2016 (US$317 million).

The Latin American countries registered important growth in crowdfunding adoption. The total transaction amount grew by 160% in 2017 with respect to 2016. Brazil with US$216.4 million invested in 2017, overtook Mexico and Chile (respectively US$151.1 million and US$150.7 million). Among the LAC, Brazil is the biggest market (33% market share), followed by Mexico (23%), Chile (23%), and the rest of region (21%) (see Figure 4.15).

In terms of most frequent crowdfunding models, in the America region (similar to Europe) investors prefer lending-based crowdfunding forms (Ziegler et al., 2018a), followed by reward-based and equity-based investment models (see Figure 4.16).

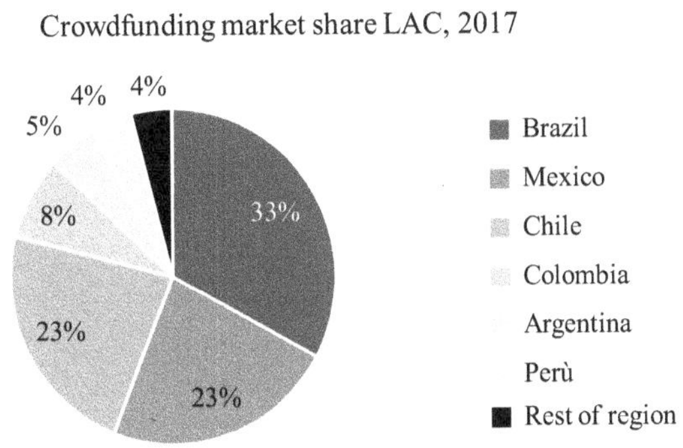

FIGURE 4.15 Crowdfunding market share: LAC, 2017

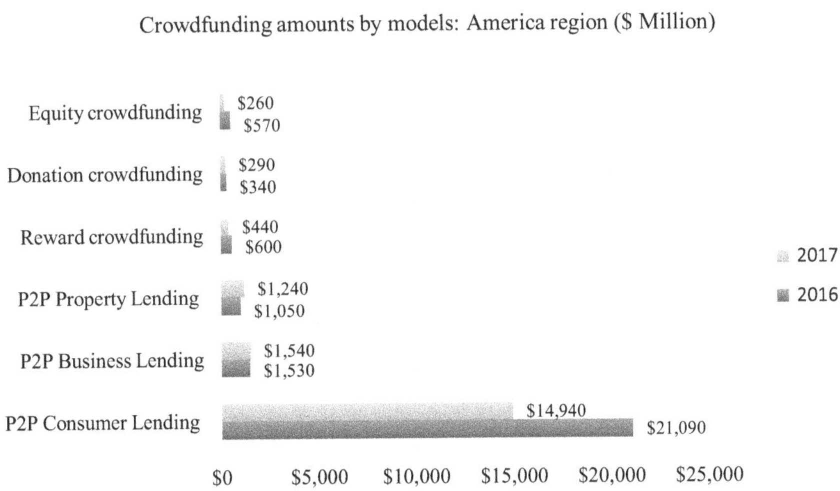

FIGURE 4.16 Crowdfunding amounts by models: America, 2016–2017

The US is ranked first for number of platforms and, also, hosts two of the best known reward crowdfunding platforms worldwide – Kickstarter and Indiegogo. Kickstarter, the most popular platform, was established in 2009 and was the first platform to operate worldwide, allowing project proponents from around the world to use the Internet and exploit the crowd to obtain financial support for their firms. Kickstarter has more than 16 million supporters and accounts for over US$4.4 billion in transaction involving more than 165,000 projects in categories such as design, technology, music, fashion, games, etc. Indiegogo began operations in 2008 in California and has more than 9 million supporters from more than 235 countries. Both platforms allow donation- and reward-based crowdfunding.

One of the most important reward-based platforms in Canada is FundRazr, which was set up in 2008. In the LAC region, Catarse is the most prominent reward-based crowdfunding platform and is based in Brazil.

4.4 The Asia Pacific market

Crowdfunding has become a viable funding option for entrepreneurs and small- and medium-sized enterprises (SMEs), which, traditionally, have reduced access to finance, especially in Asia (Ziegler et al., 2018b).

The Asia Pacific crowdfunding market was worth about US$361 billion in 2017. This area includes China, Australia, India, South-Korea, Singapore, Indonesia, and Japan. China is ranked first in this area and accounts with 99% of total Asia Pacific crowdfunding in 2017.

Adoption of crowdfunding as a financing and investment tool has grown hugely in China (see Figure 4.17) since the market was introduced in 2013. From some US$24 billion in 2014, transactions reached US$358 billion in 2017.

All the remaining countries accounting for 1% (Ziegler et al., 2018b). Australia is showing high growth rates and achieved US$1.14 billion in 2017; next ranked are South Korea (US$1.13 billion) and Japan (US$350 million). In South Asia, the most active country in the alternative finance sector is India, with a total of about US$270 million collected in 2017.

Figure 4.18 depicts the main crowdfunding models and shows that most business funding is derived from debt-based models with just over 1% of total funding based on equity- and reward-based models. Although most crowdfunding models experienced modest growth since 2015; in 2017, equity-based crowdfunding shrank by 51% ($225 million) in 2017.

Renrendai.com was founded in 2010 and is one of the largest P2P lending platforms in China. Prior to July, 2015, Chinese P2P platforms operated in an unregulated environment until the Chinese government issued some guidelines, covering ten regulatory authorities, which required online P2P lending platforms to separate investors' money by opening third-party deposit accounts in a bank supervised by the People's Bank of China and the financial regulatory authority. This regulatory framework has increased P2P lending.

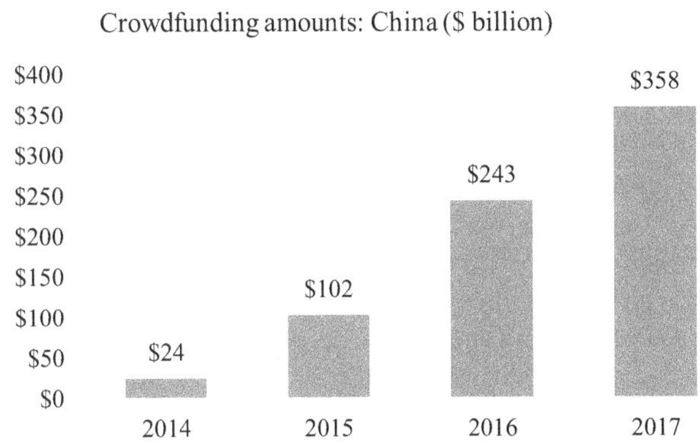

FIGURE 4.17 Crowdfunding amounts: China, 2014–2017

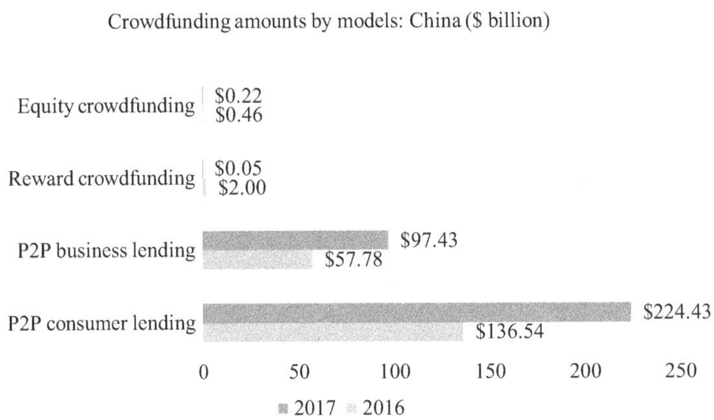

FIGURE 4.18 Crowdfunding amounts by models: China, 2016–2017

Zhongchou is a reward-based platform that was founded in China in 2013. It is a major player and targets various sectors including technology, design, events, film, and music. AngelCrunch was the first equity crowdfunding platform in China and was established in 2011.

4.5 Why does development of the crowdfunding phenomenon vary across countries?

We next analyse the contextual and cultural factors that might result in differences in crowdfunding intensity across countries. This economic activity is part of the formal and informal institutional setting. Formal institutions refer to the political, economic, and contractual rules that regulate and shape individual behaviour (e.g. North, 1990, 1991; Lowndes, 1996). Although entrepreneurial activities are mostly individual, the country context plays a role (Li and Zahra, 2012; Noorderhaven et al., 2004; Uhlaner and Thurik, 2010).

Informal institutions are the conventions, moral values, religious beliefs, and norms of behaviour that are socially diffused and are part of a country's cultural heritage (North, 1990; Pejovich, 1999). The formal institutions include the rules and government structures and the informal institutions focus on ideology and culture. Research shows that sociocultural values are an important aspect of the entrepreneurial environment and influence entrepreneurial activity and performance. Beugelsdijk (2007) and Shane (1993) show that countries with an entrepreneurial culture, which is more open to risk taking, are more successful innovators.

Formal institutions and informal cultural constraints are strongly intertwined. Formal institutions are usually embedded in the cultural setting because political, economic, and contractual rules are linked to people's understanding of how things should be done. Culture can be likened to the software of the mind (Hofstede, 1991) and formal institutions are the "products of the dominant cultural value systems" (Hofstede, 2001: 34). Therefore, the same formal institutions in societies with different cultural values can produce different economic outcomes (North, 1990).

Due to the importance of formal and informal institutions in shaping national economic activity (Hayton et al., 2002; Block et al., 2013), including entrepreneurship and access to financial resources for new ventures (Grilli et al., 2018; Li and Zahra, 2012; Bowen and De Clercq, 2008; Parker, 2018; Carree et al., 2002; Wennekers et al., 2007), we investigate these promote or hinder the adoption of crowdfunding by entrepreneurs and investors, across countries.

Using a representative sample of crowdfunding investments in 29 European countries between 2012 and 2017, we focus on the formal and informal institutions most relevant to our study context. Specifically, we consider four formal institutions, such as national entrepreneurial activity; process and cost involved in starting a business; time to export; and use of technology. We consider three informal institutions referring to cultural values, such as uncertainty avoidance, individualism, and trust, which are identified in the literature (e.g. Li and Zahra, 2012) and, especially, in country-level, comparative research on institutions.

Data on crowdfunding investments were collected from online secondary sources: crowdfunding country reports, crowdfunding platforms website and infographics, and studies mapping the alternative finance sector, published by the Cambridge Centre for Alternative finance at Judge Business School (e.g. Ziegler et al., 2018a, 2018b, 2019). Data on country-level formal institutions, such as Total Entrepreneurship Activity (TEA), business start-up costs, and the Internet use, were collected from EUROSTAT, the World Bank's World Development Indicators (WDI) database, and the Global Entrepreneurship Monitor (GEM).

Cultural dimensions, such as uncertainty avoidance and individualism versus collectivism, are from Hofstede (2001), which is a commonly used framework for studying national culture (Taras et al., 2010). Hofstede's dimensions are based on data gathered between 1967 and 1973, in 20 languages, from over 88,000 employees in a large multinational organisation, active in 72 countries. We also exploit data on trust from the 2012 and 2016 waves of the European Value Survey (EVS).

Table 4.1 presents information on the countries included in the sample.

TABLE 4.1 Countries in the sample and their characteristics

Countries				
Austria	Estonia	Iceland	Norway	Spain
Belgium	Finland	Ireland	Poland	Sweden
Bulgaria	France	Italy	Portugal	Switzerland
Croatia	Germany	Latvia	Romania	Netherlands
Czech Republic	Greece	Lithuania	Slovakia	UK
Denmark	Hungary	Luxemburg	Slovenia	

Formal and Informal institutions (average 2013–2017 of the countries listed above)

	Mean	*Std. Dev.*	*Min*	*Max*
Crowdfunding investment per capita	7.6	15.6	0	107
TEA	8%	3%	3%	19%
Ease of doing business	32.81	17	3	72
Digital literacy	81.3	11.5	54.1	98
Time to export (days)	10.7	3.9	6	20
Protection of minority shareholders	6.3	0.9	4	8
Uncertainty avoidance	67.5	20.9	23	100
Individualism	61.5	17.1	27	89
Trust	39%	18%	12%	75%

The per capita average invested in Europe on crowdfunding platforms, over the years 2013 to 2017 is 7.63 euro. The most active countries registered 107 euro of investment per capita in the same period considered. TEA is the percentage of working age population engaged in entrepreneurial activity. On average, in 2013 to 2017 in Europe, 8% of the working age population started a business; in Estonia and Latvia the percentages were 19 and 15, respectively. Ease of doing business (an index that ranks countries against each other) captures the administrative issues related to starting a business and is based on 11 indicators of business friendliness. A high value indicates an administratively cumbersome procedure involved in setting up a new business. The average ranking for European countries is 33, with the most business-friendly countries scoring 3 (Denmark) and 7 (Norway).

Digital literacy, which is the ability to use information technology and the Internet, and the frequency of their use. In Europe, digital literacy levels are high: on average, 82% of the population aged over 15 years are able to use information technologies and the Internet, and use them daily. The variable time to export refers to the number of days required to comply with the bureaucracy related to exporting. The average time in Europe is 11 days.

Average uncertainty avoidance across the respondents in a single country provides a cultural variable, which captures how individuals perceive risk taking in uncertain situations. Higher values of uncertainty avoidance indicate that the population of a particular country is less risk tolerant – which applies to Portugal, Greece, Czech Republic, and Poland. Low values indicate higher tolerance of risk and apply to the UK, the Netherlands, and the Northern European countries. Individualism captures the degree to which the population prefers to act as individuals rather than members of a group (Hofstede, 1994). A higher score for this dimension implies that the society is more individualistic – which applies to the UK, the Netherlands, Hungary, and Italy. Last, trust captures the percentage of people who believe that most people can be trusted. On average, in Europe, 39% of the populations of the countries analysed, trust others, although the score is lower in Bulgaria, Croatia, Portugal, and Romania and higher (almost 70% of the population) in Norway, Finland, and Denmark.

In Sections 4.5.1 and 4.5.2, we discuss the effects the above described formal and informal institutions on crowdfunding activity across European countries.

4.5.1 The influence of formal institutional characteristics on crowdfunding development

Countries differ in their regulation and institutions (Audretsch et al., 2007; Nicoletti and Pryor, 2006) and the level of bureaucracy involved in setting up a new venture (Djankov et al., 2002; Grilo and Irigoyen, 2006; Levie and Autio, 2011).

Drawing on the existing literature, among the many formal institutional characteristics that might influence the development of crowdfunding across countries, we focus on the roles of: (i) the country's entrepreneurial activity; (ii) ease of doing business; (iii) time to export; and (iv) use of technology.

4.5.1.1 Entrepreneurial activity

Among the different early-stage funding options, crowdfunding is important for the growth and survival of many start-ups because entrepreneurs tend to be credit constrained (Evans and Leighton, 1990; Stinchcombe, 1965) and banks often are reluctant to invest without collateral (Wright and Robbie, 1998). Therefore, the level of entrepreneurial activity in the country shall have a positive influence on the demand for crowdfunding investment. We measure entrepreneurial activity by TEA, which is the percentage of working-age population actively involved in business start-up activity, either immediately before firm establishment (nascent entrepreneurs) or in the 42 months after the birth of the firm. These data are available from GEM. Figure 4.19 reports the univariate regression between the average crowdfunding investment per capita and entrepreneurial activity for each county on which we have data.

The graph shows a positive relationship between the country's level of entrepreneurial activity and the amount invested via crowdfunding platforms.

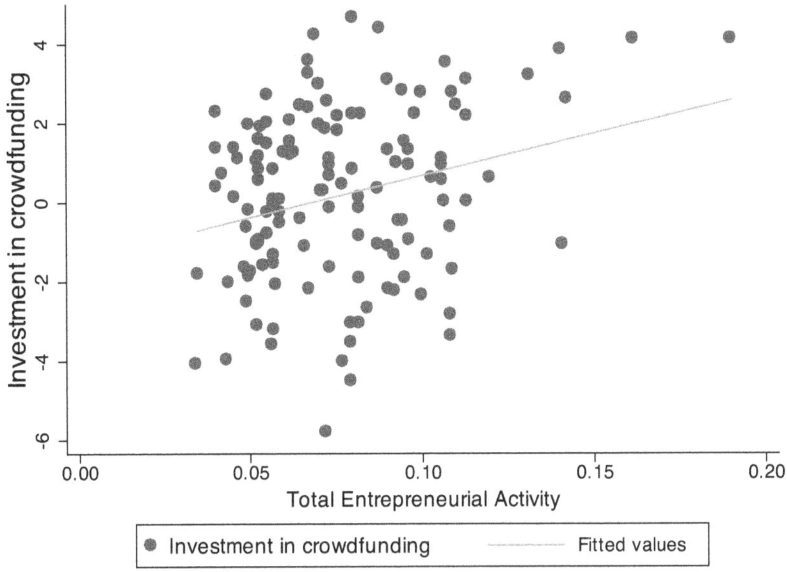

FIGURE 4.19 Crowdfunding and TEA

It shows that, in countries where the population is more actively involved in entrepreneurial activities, demand for investment is higher and, thus, the per capita amount invested in entrepreneurial ventures during the years considered is higher compared to countries with lower levels of entrepreneurial activity.

4.5.1.2 Ease of doing business

The level of regulation and the administrative steps required to set up a business have an effect on entrepreneurship activity. For instance, studies show that minimum capital requirements and labour market regulation affect entrepreneurship (Van Stel et al., 2007). Also, less burdensome regulation is associated to a higher number of nascent or new entrepreneurs (Levie and Autio, 2011). Comparing data for Spain (a heavily regulated economy) and the UK (a lightly regulated economy), Capelleras et al. (2008) show that newly registered firms in the UK are smaller in size and grow more quickly than newly registered firms in Spain.

In line with this, we expect that high levels of administrative and regulatory complexity involved in setting up a business, will discourage entrepreneurial activity, which, in turn, will affect the use of crowdfunding as a financing tool.

To investigate this relationship, we employ a measure for ease of doing business, developed by the World Bank,[3] which captures several business regulation indicators such as the administrative procedures required to start a business, average time and cost, minimum capital required to establish a limited liability company. This index also includes procedures, time and cost to complete the formalities required for construction permits (e.g. to build a warehouse, including electricity supply and property registration); the access to credit and the strength of minority shareholders' rights in related-party transactions and in corporate governance, which is scored on a 0–10 scale. On average, minority shareholders are fairly well protected in Europe, although in some countries, such as Switzerland and Hungary, the score is below the average of 6.3, while the UK, Sweden, and Ireland score 7.5.

The time required to arrange the export of a product is also important as is the country's taxation regime, both captured by the index.

Overall, the ranking for ease of doing business provides information on the performance of the economy on business regulation relative to the performance of other economies. Countries scoring 1 being the most business friendly and countries scoring 60 or 70 or lower being countries with very complex administrative and regulatory procedures related to starting a business.

Figure 4.20 reports the univariate regression between average per capita crowdfunding investment and ease of doing business, for each county on which we have data.

The graph shows that more complex administrative and regulatory procedures related to starting a business discourage entrepreneurship, and thus the use of crowdfunding.

On the other hand, business-friendly countries like in the UK, Denmark, Norway, Sweden, or Estonia will have higher chances that individual will start their own business and it translates in higher use of crowdfunding as financing tool.

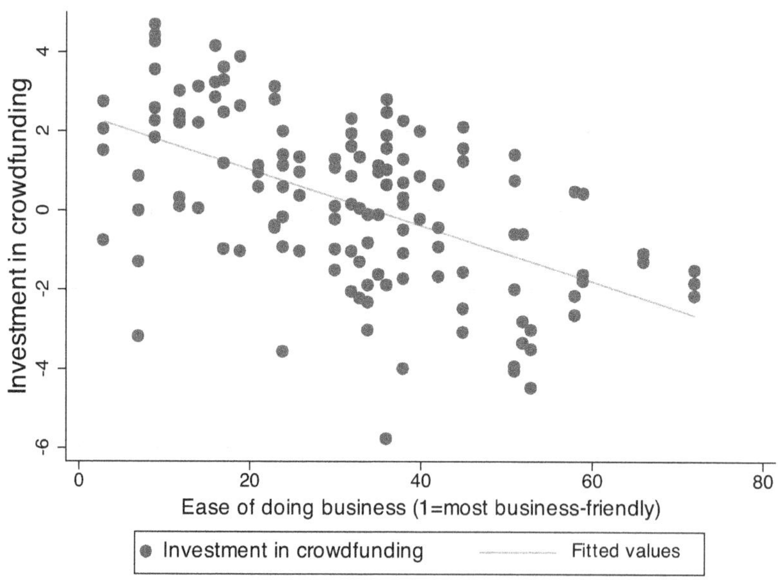

FIGURE 4.20 Crowdfunding and ease of doing business

4.5.1.3 Time to export

Time to export refers to the time necessary to comply with all procedures required to export goods. The measure used for time to export was developed by the World Bank and considers the time, in calendar days, from the moment the procedures starts to their completion. It is important to consider how the efficiency of the export procedures affects the use of crowdfunding by entrepreneurs and investors. Some forms of crowdfunding, such as reward-based crowdfunding, require the entrepreneur to announce a target shipping date of their product if the fundraising goal is met. Backers from around the world pledge money in exchange for rewards such as one of the items being created: albums, films, games, and gadgets are especially popular. For these entrepreneurs, an efficient logistics infrastructure is important to allow timely delivery of the reward to backers. Previous work on crowdfunding shows that more than 75% receive the product later than expected (Mollick, 2014) and suggest that this delay might be due to there being a large number of backers, failure on the part of the entrepreneur to estimate the number of rewards required, and extensive projects involving complex coordination and planning (Brown and Eisenhardt, 1995; Rothwell et al., 1974). Delayed delivery can constitute a negative signal about the company, such as the inability of the entrepreneur to plan accurately, to meet expectation, or execute a task. We believe that countries with less efficient logistics infrastructure will discourage project proponents and entrepreneurs from using crowdfunding, to avoid negative signals to the market.

Figure 4.21 reports the univariate regression between the average per capita crowdfunding investment and the time required to export goods, for all the countries on which we have data.

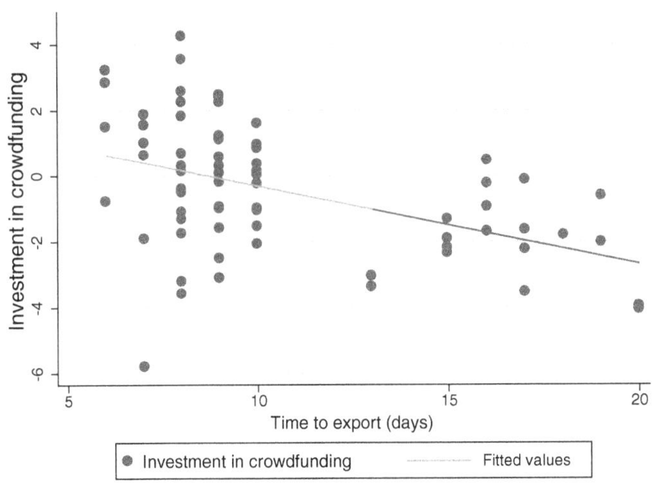

FIGURE 4.21 Crowdfunding and time to export

The graph shows that there is a negative relationship between the time required to export goods and the level of crowdfunding activity in the country. In other words, the longer and more cumbersome the export procedures, the lower the use of crowdfunding by the country's entrepreneurs, who are discouraged by the inefficiency of the logistics infrastructure which might reduce their ability to meet customers' and backers' expectations.

4.5.1.4 Use of technology and digital literacy

Digital literacy refers to the ability of individuals to use digital technologies. Crowdfunding is facilitated by technology and the development of Web 2.0 technologies has facilitated interactions via the Internet. Crowdfunding relies on online interactions between fundraisers and investors, facilitated by online platforms (Eisenmann et al., 2009). Therefore, familiarity with use of the internet has an important influence on the development of crowdfunding. A good proxy for individual digital literacy is frequency of Internet access, online purchase, and personal computer use. Specifically, the country level indicators employed measure the percentage of individuals using both a personal computer and the Internet on a daily basis, and the percentage of individuals who purchased online items during the immediate previous three months. Data were extracted from World Development Indicators (WDI) database, available online from the World Bank website (databank.worldbank.org).

Figure 4.22 reports the univariate regression between the average crowdfunding investment per capita and the level of digital literacy for each county for which we have data.

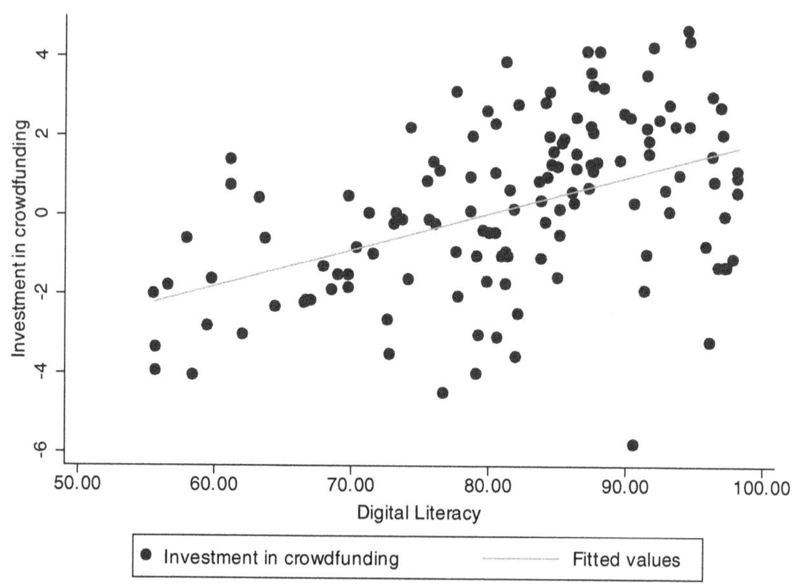

FIGURE 4.22 Crowdfunding and digital literacy

The graph shows that the average per-capita amount invested in crowdfunding in each country, is influenced positively by the level of digital literacy in that country. In countries where most of the population (90% or more) use digital technologies and the Internet every day and, therefore, are familiar with their use, there is a higher likelihood of using digital financing tools, such as crowdfunding, to support entrepreneurial activity or raise funding from the crowd. Countries with lower levels of digital literacy are less likely to use crowdfunding for investment.

4.5.2 The influence of informal institutional characteristics on crowdfunding development

There is a large body of work on the role of informal institutions in shaping economic behaviour. As already mentioned, informal institutions include conventions, moral values, religious beliefs, and norms of behaviour which are part of a country's culture heritage (North, 1990; Pejovich, 1999).

Several studies investigate the influence of informal institutions on various economic activities, including modes of employment (Hofstede et al., 2004), entrepreneurial potential (Mueller and Thomas, 2001; Zhao et al., 2010), innovation championing strategies (Shane, 1992), international technology alliances (Steensma et al., 2000), debt maturity structure (Zheng et al., 2012), knowledge sharing (Möller and Svahn, 2004), and venture capital activity (Li and Zahra, 2012).

We examine the influence of informal institutions on the development of crowdfunding across countries, focusing on three characteristics which have been shown to influence entrepreneurship and investment activities (Li and Zahra, 2012): (i) individual tendency to avoid uncertainty; (ii) individualism attitudes (Hofstede et al., 1990); and (iii) trusting in others.

Uncertainty avoidance, individualism, and trust are informal institutions relevant to the investment decision since they express the propensity to avoid uncertainty, reduce information asymmetry, and opportunistic behaviour, all elements that characterise investment in entrepreneurial ventures via crowdfunding platforms (Ahlers et al., 2015; Baum and Silverman, 2004; Vismara, 2018).

4.5.2.1 Uncertainty avoidance

Uncertainty avoidance refers to the extent a society feels comfortable or uncomfortable with unknown, surprising, and different-from-usual situations (Hofstede, 1994). Some societies are more anxious than others about the unpredictability of the future and, thus, are less likely to engage in risk-taking activities. Uncertainty avoidance affects crowdfunding in two ways. From the project proponent's perspective, the intensity of crowdfunding may be influenced by the extent to which the society is willing to engage in risk-taking activities such as starting a new business or engaging in an innovative project. Previous research confirms that uncertainty-avoiding societies are characterised by less entrepreneurial activity (Mueller and Thomas, 2001; Shane, 1995; Zhao et al., 2010). Also, considering the uncertainty associated to survival and performance of a new venture, more risk averse countries and societies, sensitive to public judgment about success as an entrepreneur (House et al., 2004), will be less likely to present a new businesses or innovative project to the public for financing via a crowdfunding platform.

From an investors' perspective, use of crowdfunding may be influenced by the individual willingness to invest disposable income in a highly uncertain project. Also, information asymmetry between investors and project initiator can lead to inaccurate assessment of the value of the project (Ahlers et al., 2015; Baum and Silverman, 2004; Dewally and Ederington, 2006; Vismara, 2018) and increase the risks related to investing in a crowdfunding project.

To measure the level of uncertainty avoidance, we employ Hofstede's (1980) index, which is on a scale from 1 to 100, reflecting the degree to which society feels threatened by ambiguous or unknown situations. Although Hofstede's cultural dimensions were developed in the 1960s and 1970s, these measures are considered standard tools for cultural research (see, e.g. Li and Zahra, 2012; Shane, 1992; Steensma et al., 2000; Crossland and Hambrick, 2011). National culture is fairly stable over time and a country's uncertainty avoidance and individualism scores represent its position relative to other countries – and this rarely shifts.

Figure 4.23 depicts the univariate regression between average per capita crowdfunding investment and uncertainty avoidance in each country for which we have data.

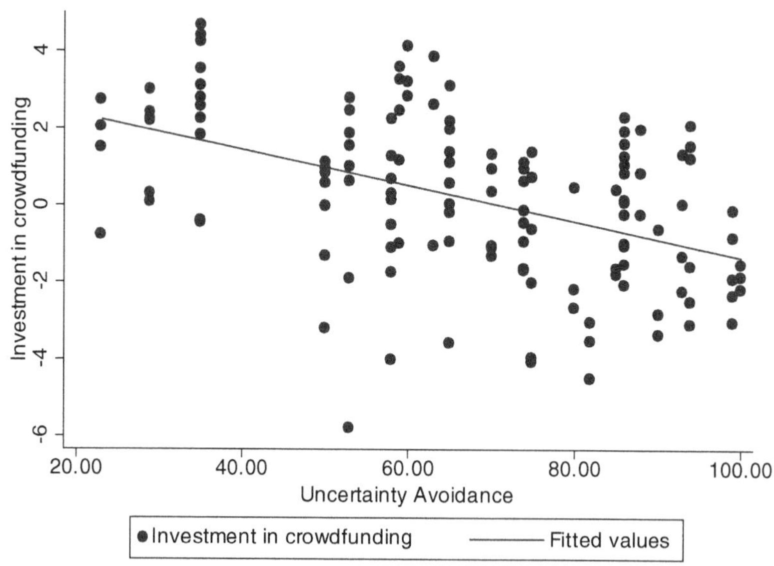

FIGURE 4.23 Crowdfunding and uncertainty avoidance

The graph shows a negative trend between countries' uncertainty avoidance and crowdfunding investments. In other words, in countries where people are more averse to uncertainty, there is a tendency to invest less and to use crowdfunding less for financing purposes. We can assume that, from an investor perspective, crowdfunding investments are seen as risky due to the uncertainty of early-stage business and the difficulty involved in evaluating their potential (Zhang and Liu, 2012). On the other hand, uncertainty averse societies are characterised by less entrepreneurial activity (Mueller and Thomas, 2001; Shane, 1995), therefore, demand for crowd investing will be lower.

4.5.2.2 Individualism attitudes

Individualistic cultures are societies in which the ties between individuals are loose (Hofstede, 1991), whereas collectivistic cultures are societies where individuals, from birth, are integrated into strong, cohesive in-groups (Hofstede, 1991). Collectivist societies are bounded by informal relationships built on common values, norms, and collective goals (Etzioni, 1968); they rely more on informal relationships to mitigate information asymmetries and transaction costs (Gould, 1993). Individualist societies rely heavily on formal institutions, such as political, economic, and contractual rules, to reduce transaction costs and promote economic transactions (Steensma et al., 2000; Tiessen, 1997); they are motivated strongly by personal achievement (Hayton et al., 2002), are more innovative (Shane, 1992), and entrepreneurial (Mueller and Thomas, 2001).

In crowdfunding, as an online form of financing, personal interaction between entrepreneurs and investors is uncommon and the possibility to forge informal relationship between fundraisers and investors to reduce transaction costs, is small. Therefore, collectivistic societies may be discouraged from investing in crowdfunding. On the other hand, individualistic societies, which are more entrepreneurially oriented, may find crowdfunding appealing. We test our conjectures using the individualism and collectivism measures developed by Hofstede (1980), scored on a 1–100 scale for degree of interdependence among society's members.

Figure 4.24 reports the univariate regression between average crowdfunding investment per capita and the individualism scores for each country for which we have data.

The graph shows that, the average per-capita amount invested in crowdfunding in each country is positively influenced by the country's level individualism. Individualistic societies, which are more entrepreneurially oriented (Mueller and Thomas, 2001), are more open to using digital financing tools, such as crowdfunding, to support entrepreneurial activities or raise funding from the crowd, compared to collectivistic societies.

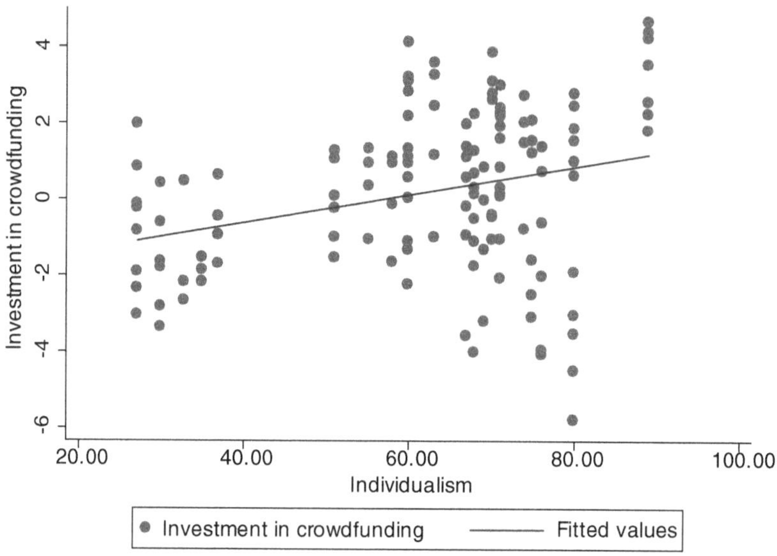

FIGURE 4.24 Crowdfunding and individualism attitudes

4.5.2.3 Trust

Trust has been shown to be important for determining economic activity. Higher levels of trust are associated to higher levels of economic growth (Knack and Keefer, 1997), higher levels of financial development (Guiso et al., 2004, 2008), and higher levels of international trade and investment (Guiso et al., 2009).

We investigate the influence of trust on the adoption of crowdfunding across countries. A high level of trust affects the investment process by reducing moral hazard and transaction costs (Bottazzi et al., 2016; Hain et al., 2016; Grilli et al., 2018). Several studies document the effect of trust on the financial decisions of both individuals and firms (Guiso et al., 2008; Bottazzi et al., 2016). Also, crowdfunding contracts are less complex since the stakes per individual investor typically are lower and the relationship is based more on "online trust" than on contractual conditions (Schwienbacher and Larralde, 2010). Therefore, the propensity to trust others is particularly relevant in the case of crowdfunding. Crowdfunding relies on online interactions between entrepreneur and investors, and the latter need to be able to trust the information disclosed by the entrepreneur regarding his or her capacity to run the business and develop a new idea. The level of information asymmetry is high as is the risk of moral hazard (Ahlers et al., 2015; Vismara, 2018). Since customers commit funds before the entrepreneur invests in production, the entrepreneur has the possibility of shirking or embezzling the funds and not delivering the promised reward (Strausz, 2017; Lin and Pursiainen, 2018). Therefore, individuals who trust other people will be more likely to invest in novel ideas proposed by entrepreneurs wanting to set up an innovative firm. This could lead to a higher intensity of early stage investment via crowdfunding platforms.

We test our conjecture using data on trust across Europe extracted from the European Value Study, a cross-national survey of basic human values. It provides insights into the ideas, beliefs, preferences, attitudes, values, and opinions of European citizens. The data are available online from the European Value Study website (europeanvaluesstudy.eu). The responses to the question capture expectations about others' trustworthiness.

Figure 4.25 reports the univariate regression between average per capita crowdfunding investment and the country's trust score for those countries for which we have data.

Our results suggest a positive influence of level of trust in others, on the level of the country's crowdfunding activity. Trust mitigates moral hazard problems and, therefore, facilitates crowdfunding use and performance. Previous research suggests that individual willingness to sign a financial contract depends not only on the enforceability of contracts, but also on the extent to which they trust the counterpart (Guiso et al., 2004, 2008).

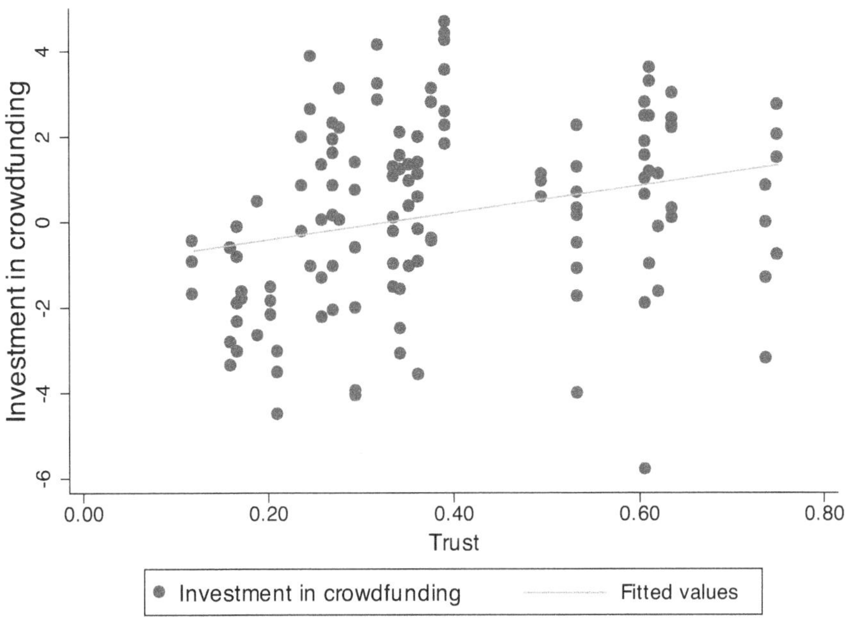

FIGURE 4.25 Crowdfunding and trust

4.6 Final reflections

Crowdfunding plays an important role in funding new ventures and has become a significant source of economic and technological development. Little empirical evidence exists on what causes the variability in crowdfunding activity across countries. In this chapter, we explored how the development of crowdfunding varies across countries and the impact of national formal and informal institutional characteristics on its use.

We showed that there continue to be substantial differences in crowdfunding activity both between European and non-European countries, and among EU member states. China was shown to be the biggest crowdfunding market, followed by the US and Europe. Within Europe, the UK is the leader, followed by France and Germany. In terms of crowdfunding types, across countries, P2P lending crowdfunding is the most frequent, while equity crowdfunding, although increasing, is a small proportion of the entire market.

Countries' formal and informal institutional developments have a significant impact on the discrepancies in levels of crowdfunding activity. Countries with more conducive business environments record higher levels of crowdfunding. Reducing the costs for local firms to do business enhances their efficiency and competitiveness, and encourages investment. Improving public administration and making business procedures more transparent and efficient, would encourage business creation and investment, which are critical for economic growth.

The level of crowdfunding activity depends, also, on informal institutions, including social norms, culture, trust, and the individual attitude to business creation and early stage investment (North, 1990). Societies characterised by low-risk aversion and an individualistic attitude tend to be more prone to use crowdfunding to finance their businesses and to invest in early stage companies via these platforms. Also, societies that are more trusting of others are more likely to fund novel ideas.

The influence of culture acts as a guide to the assessment of the need for training in different culture setting. Countries characterised by high levels of uncertainty avoidance may need incentives to stimulate crowdfunding activity, in the form, for instance, of a strong formal institutional framework.

This study adds to the recommendations related to appropriate policy frameworks to facilitate access to funding and other resources, and promote entrepreneurial activity (Lerner, 2000).

Notes

1 https://ec.europa.eu/info/business-economy-euro/growth-and-investment/financing-investment/crowdfunding_en

2 Latin American Countries (LAC) include: Anguilla, Antigua & Barbuda, Argentina, Barbados, Belize, Bermuda, Bolivia, Brazil, Canada, Chile, Colombia, Costa Rica, Cuba, Curacao, Dominica, Dominican Republic, Ecuador, El Salvador, the Falkland

Islands (Malvinas), Guam, Guatemala, Haiti, Honduras, Jamaica, Mexico, Nicaragua, Panama, Paraguay, Peru, Puerto Rico, Saint Lucia, Suriname, Trinidad and Tobago, Uruguay, Venezuela.

3 https://www.doingbusiness.org/en/reports/global-reports/doing-business-2019

References

Ahlers, G.K., Cumming, D., Günther, C. and Schweizer, D., 2015. Signaling in equity crowdfunding. *Entrepreneurship Theory and Practice*, *39*(4), pp. 955–980.

Audretsch, D.B., Grilo, I. and Thurik, A.R. eds., 2007. *Handbook of Research on Entrepreneurship Policy*. Edward Elgar Publishing, Cheltenham.

Beugelsdijk, S., 2007. Entrepreneurial culture, regional innovativeness and economic growth. *Journal of Evolutionary Economics*, *17*(2), pp. 187–210.

Baum, J.A. and Silverman, B.S., 2004. Picking winners or building them? Alliance, intellectual, and human capital as selection criteria in venture financing and performance of biotechnology startups. *Journal of Business Venturing*, *19*(3), pp. 411–436.

Block, J., Thurik, A.R., Van der Zwan, P. and Walter, S., 2013. Business takeover or new venture start? Individual and environmental determinants from a cross-country study. *Entrepreneurship: Theory and Practice*, *37*, pp. 1099–1121.

Bottazzi, L., Da Rin, M. and Hellmann, T., 2016. The importance of trust for investment: Evidence from venture capital. *The Review of Financial Studies*, *29*(9), pp. 2283–2318.

Bowen, H.P. and De Clercq, D., 2008. Institutional context and the allocation of entrepreneurial effort. *Journal of International Business Studies*, *39*(4), pp. 747–767.

Brown, S.L. and Eisenhardt, K.M., 1995. Product development: Past research, present findings, and future directions. *Academy of Management Review*, *20*(2), pp. 343–378.

Capelleras, J.L., Mole, K.F., Greene, F.J. and Storey, D.J., 2008. Do more heavily regulated economies have poorer performing new ventures? Evidence from Britain and Spain. *Journal of International Business Studies*, *39*(4), pp. 688–704.

Carree, M., Van Stel, A., Thurik, R. and Wennekers, S., 2002. Economic development and business ownership: An analysis using data of 23 OECD countries in the period 1976–1996. *Small Business Economics*, *19*(3), pp. 271–290.

Crossland, C. and Hambrick, D.C., 2011. Differences in managerial discretion across countries: How nation-level institutions affect the degree to which CEOs matter. *Strategic Management Journal*, *32*(8), pp. 797–819.

Dewally, M. and Ederington, L., 2006. Reputation, certification, warranties, and information as remedies for seller-buyer information asymmetries: Lessons from the online comic book market. *The Journal of Business*, *79*(2), pp. 693–729.

Djankov, S., La Porta, R., Lopez-de-Silanes, F. and Shleifer, A., 2002. The regulation of entry. *The Quarterly Journal of Economics*, *117*(1), pp. 1–37.

Eisenmann, T.R., Parker, G. and Van Alstyne, M., 2009. Opening platforms: How, when and why? *Platforms, Markets and Innovation*, *6*, pp. 131–162.

Etzioni, A., 1968. *The Active Society*. Free Press, New York, NY.

Evans, D.S. and Leighton, L.S., 1990. Some empirical aspects of entrepreneurship. In *The Economics of Small Firms* (pp. 79–99). Springer, Dordrecht, the Netherlands.

Gould, R.V., 1993. Collective action and network structure. *American Sociological Review*, *58*, pp. 182–196.

Grilli, L., Mrkajic, B. and Latifi, G., 2018. Venture capital in Europe: Social capital, formal institutions and mediation effects. *Small Business Economics*, *51*(2), pp. 393–410.

Grilo, I. and Irigoyen, J.M., 2006. Entrepreneurship in the EU: To wish and not to be. *Small Business Economics*, *26*(4), pp. 305–318.

Guiso, L., Sapienza, P. and Zingales, L., 2004. The role of social capital in financial development. *American Economic Review, 94*(3), pp. 526–556.
Guiso, L., Sapienza, P. and Zingales, L., 2008. Trusting the stock market. *The Journal of Finance, 63*(6), pp. 2557–2600.
Guiso, L., Sapienza, P. and Zingales, L., 2009. Cultural biases in economic exchange? *The Quarterly Journal of Economics, 124*(3), pp. 1095–1131.
Hain, D., Johan, S. and Wang, D., 2016. Determinants of cross-border venture capital investments in emerging and developed economies: The effects of relational and institutional trust. *Journal of Business Ethics, 138*(4), pp. 743–764.
Hayton, J.C., George, G. and Zahra, S.A., 2002. National culture and entrepreneurship: A review of behavioral research. *Entrepreneurship Theory and Practice, 26*(4), pp. 33–52.
Hofstede, G., 1980. Culture and organizations. *International Studies of Management & Organization, 10*(4), pp. 15–41.
Hofstede, G., Neuijen, B., Ohayv, D.D. and Sanders, G., 1990. Measuring organizational cultures: A qualitative and quantitative study across twenty cases. *Administrative Science Quarterly, 35*, pp. 286–316.
Hofstede, G., 1991. *Organizations and Cultures: Software of the Mind.* McGrawHill, New York.
Hofstede, G., 1994. The business of international business is culture. *International Business Review, 3*(1), pp. 1–14.
Hofstede, G., 2001. *Culture's Consequences: Comparing Values, Behaviors, Institutions and Organizations across Nations.* Sage Publications, Thousand Oaks, CA.
Hofstede, G., Noorderhaven, N.G., Thurik, A.R., Uhlaner, L.M., Wennekers, A.R. and Wildeman, R.E., 2004. Culture's role in entrepreneurship: Self-employment out of dissatisfaction. In *Innovation, Entrepreneurship and Culture: The Interaction between Technology, Progress and Economic Growth* (pp. 162–203). Edward Elgar Publishing, Cheltenham.
House, R.J., Hanges, P.J., Javidan, M., Dorfman, P.W. and Gupta, V. eds., 2004. *Culture, Leadership, and Organizations: The GLOBE Study of 62 Societies.* Sage Publications, Thousand Oaks, CA.
Knack, S. and Keefer, P., 1997. Does social capital have an economic payoff? A cross-country investigation. *The Quarterly Journal of Economics, 112*(4), pp. 1251–1288.
Lerner, J., 2000. Assessing the contribution of venture capital. *The RAND Journal of Economics, 31*(4), pp. 674–692.
Levie, J. and Autio, E., 2011. Regulatory burden, rule of law, and entry of strategic entrepreneurs: An international panel study. *Journal of Management Studies, 48*(6), pp. 1392–1419.
Li, Y. and Zahra, S.A., 2012. Formal institutions, culture, and venture capital activity: A cross-country analysis. *Journal of Business Venturing, 27*(1), pp. 95–111.
Lin, T.C. and Pursiainen, V., 2018, July 31. Fund what you trust? Social capital and moral hazard in crowdfunding. *Social Capital and Moral Hazard in Crowdfunding.*
Lowndes, V., 1996. Varieties of new institutionalism: A critical appraisal. *Public Administration, 74*(2), pp. 181–197.
Möller, K. and Svahn, S., 2004. Crossing East-West boundaries: Knowledge sharing in intercultural business networks. *Industrial Marketing Management, 33*(3), pp. 219–228.
Mollick, E., 2014. The dynamics of crowdfunding: An exploratory study. *Journal of Business Venturing, 29*(1), pp. 1–16.
Mueller, S.L. and Thomas, A.S., 2001. Culture and entrepreneurial potential: A nine country study of locus of control and innovativeness. *Journal of Business Venturing, 16*(1), pp. 51–75.

Nicoletti, G. and Pryor, F.L., 2006. Subjective and objective measures of governmental regulations in OECD nations. *Journal of Economic Behavior & Organization, 59*(3), pp. 433–449.

Noorderhaven, N., Thurik, R., Wennekers, S. and Van Stel, A., 2004. The role of dissatisfaction and per capita income in explaining self-employment across 15 European countries. *Entrepreneurship Theory and Practice, 28*(5), pp. 447–466.

North, D., 1990. *Institutions, Institutional Change and Economic Performance*. Cambridge University Press, Cambridge.

North, D.C., 1991. Institutions. *Journal of Economic Perspectives, 5*(1), pp. 97–112.

Parker, S.C., 2018. *The Economics of Entrepreneurship*. Cambridge University Press, London.

Pejovich, S., 1999. The effects of the interaction of formal and informal institutions on social stability and economic development. *Journal of Markets & Morality, 2*(2), pp. 164–181.

Rothwell, R., Freeman, C., Horlsey, A., Jervis, V.T.P., Robertson, A.B. and Townsend, J., 1974. SAPPHO updated-project SAPPHO phase II. *Research Policy, 3*(3), pp. 258–291.

Schwienbacher, A. and Larralde, B., 2012. Crowdfunding of small entrepreneurial ventures. In Cumming, D. (ed.), *The Oxford Handbook of Entrepreneurial Finance*. Oxford University Press, Oxford.

Shane, S., 1993. Cultural influences on national rates of innovation. *Journal of Business Venturing, 8*(1), pp. 59–73.

Shane, S., 1995. August. Is the independent entrepreneurial firm a valuable organizational form? In *Academy of Management Proceedings* (Vol. 1995, No. 1, pp. 110–113). Academy of Management, Briarcliff Manor, NY.

Shane, S.A., 1992. Why do some societies invent more than others? *Journal of Business Venturing*, 7(1), pp. 29–46.

Steensma, H.K., Marino, L., Weaver, K.M. and Dickson, P.H., 2000. The influence of national culture on the formation of technology alliances by entrepreneurial firms. *Academy of Management Journal, 43*(5), pp. 951–973.

Stinchcombe, A., 1965. Social structure and organizations. In March, J.G. (ed.), *Handbook of Organizations* (pp. 142–193). Rand McNally and Company, Chicago, IL.

Strausz, R., 2017. A theory of crowdfunding: A mechanism design approach with demand uncertainty and moral hazard. *American Economic Review, 107*(6), pp. 1430–1476.

Taras, V., Kirkman, B.L. and Steel, P., 2010. Examining the impact of culture's consequences: A three-decade, multilevel, meta-analytic review of Hofstede's cultural value dimensions. *Journal of Applied Psychology, 95*(3), p. 405.

Tiessen, J.H., 1997. Individualism, collectivism, and entrepreneurship: A framework for international comparative research. *Journal of Business Venturing, 12*(5), pp. 367–384.

Uhlaner, L. and Thurik, R., 2010. Postmaterialism influencing total entrepreneurial activity across nations. In *Entrepreneurship and Culture* (pp. 301–328). Springer, Berlin, Germany.

Van Stel, A., Storey, D.J. and Thurik, A.R., 2007. The effect of business regulations on nascent and young business entrepreneurship. *Small Business Economics, 28*(2–3), pp. 171–186.

Vismara, S., 2018. Information cascades among investors in equity crowdfunding. *Entrepreneurship Theory and Practice, 42*(3), pp. 467–497.

Wennekers, S., Thurik, R., van Stel, A. and Noorderhaven, N., 2007. Uncertainty avoidance and the rate of business ownership across 21 OECD countries, 1976–2004. *Journal of Evolutionary Economics, 17*(2), pp. 133–160.

Wright, M. and Robbie, K., 1998. Venture capital and private equity: A review and synthesis. *Journal of Business Finance & Accounting, 25*(5 & 6), pp. 521–570.

Zhang, J. and Liu, P., 2012. Rational herding in microloan markets. *Management Science, 58*(5), pp. 892–912.

Zhao, H., Seibert, S.E. and Lumpkin, G.T., 2010. The relationship of personality to entrepreneurial intentions and performance: A meta-analytic review. *Journal of Management*, *36*(2), pp. 381–404.

Zheng, X., El Ghoul, S., Guedhami, O. and Kwok, C.C., 2012. National culture and corporate debt maturity. *Journal of Banking & Finance*, *36*(2), pp. 468–488.

Ziegler, D.J., King, M., Zhang, B., Mammadova, L., Ferri, F., Trappe, R., Suresh, K., Hao, R., Ryll, L. and Yerolemou, N., 2018a. *Reaching New Heights: The 3rd Americas Alternative Finance Industry Report*. University of Cambridge, Cambridge Centre for Alternative Finance.

Ziegler, D.J., Zhang, B., Shenglin, B., Wang, W., Mammadova, L., Hao, R., Luo, D. et al., 2018b. *The 3rd Asia Pacific Region Alternative Finance Industry Report*. University of Cambridge, Cambridge Centre for Alternative Finance.

Ziegler, T., Shneor, R., Wenzlaff, K., Odorović, A., Johanson, D., Hao, R. and Ryll, L., 2019. *4th European Alternative Finance Benchmarking Report*. University of Cambridge, Cambridge Centre for Alternative Finance.

PART II

Deciphering equity crowdfunding

Following the general introduction to crowdfunding, Part II of this book investigates the phenomenon of equity crowdfunding in more depth. Chapter 5 offers a general discussion of equity crowdfunding in Europe, highlighting its advantages and disadvantages for entrepreneurs and investors. Chapter 6 examines the post-funding phase and how entrepreneurs can leverage the crowd to obtain additional benefits such as knowledge and networks. Chapter 7 provides empirical evidence on the performance of crowd-backed companies and how crowdfunding has enabled access to further finance.

5

EQUITY CROWDFUNDING

Benefits and risks for entrepreneurs and investors

Following a general description of the equity crowdfunding phenomenon in Europe, Chapter 5 provides an in-depth analysis of the two market leading platforms in the UK, Crowdcube and Seedrs, highlighting their characteristics and main differences. Based on an original qualitative dataset of UK companies that have used equity crowdfunding, this chapter discusses the advantages and disadvantages for entrepreneurs and investors approaching crowdfunding.

5.1 How equity crowdfunding works

Equity crowdfunding can be defined as a financing method involving the entrepreneur selling shares in the company to a group of (small) investors through an open call for funding on an Internet-based platform (Ahlers et al., 2015). It represents an alternative source of funding for start-ups and small and medium-sized enterprises (SMEs) that regulators have been considering when formulating their economic development policies for small businesses (Cumming et al., 2016). Since 2012, the popularity of equity crowdfunding has increased hugely in the UK and the US as an innovative way for companies to raise funding. This has resulted in the democratisation of finance, which is allowing small- and medium-sized investors to purchase shares in the types of companies that, previously, were confined to professional investors such as private equity or venture capital companies.

However, these offers of unlisted companies' shares to the general public have provoked regulatory intervention to mitigate the risks for investors and protect them against potential fraudulent behaviour.

Thus, the development of equity crowdfunding across countries is linked to the role of local governments and regulators in promoting or impeding its use among entrepreneurs and investors. Several steps have been taken to remove the obstacles to crowdfunding and ensure greater operability. Initially, only a few European countries allowed start-ups to sell equity instruments to small investors via platforms; however, most countries now have efficient rules in place to incentivise the use of alternative sources of equity financing.

In the US, the focus on equity crowdfunding was justified mainly by the need to boost economic growth and job creation following the 2008 financial crisis. To facilitate access to capital for early stage companies, in 2011, President Barak Obama announced the Start-Up America Initiative, which became known as the 2012 Jumpstart Our Business Startups or JOBS Act. The JOBS act was implemented in 2013 and significantly increased small venture entrepreneurs' access to raising finance. In the European equity crowdfunding market, the UK has the most developed market (Vismara, 2018) and has held the largest market share since the 2012 (see Section 4.2 for an overview the crowdfunding market in Europe). This rapid development is due to the incentives introduced by the UK regulator to boost adoption of this financial tool by both investors and entrepreneurs and boost economic growth in the UK by promoting new the formation of new enterprises and entrepreneurship. The Enterprise Investment Scheme (EIS), introduced in the UK in 1994, offers tax benefits to investors in return for investment in small and early stage start-up businesses, with maximum employment of 250 and gross assets of £15 million. The Seed Enterprise Investment Scheme (SEIS) was introduced in 2012. It is similar to the EIS, but is designed to allow investment in very small companies (with less than 50 staff members and a £200,000 gross assets) in the UK.[1] Other European countries have followed the example of the UK, although the amounts of capital raised in these other countries in 2014–2017 is far behind the total raised in the UK.

Crowdfunding is open to any entrepreneur willing to share business plans to try to obtain funding, but there are certain restrictions on investors. Investing in private or unlisted companies can be rewarding, but involves a level of risk which investors need to be aware of. Early-stage or private companies may not perform in line with the financial projections or forecasts made during the crowdfunding campaign and investors in early-stage companies may have to wait a considerable time to see any return on their investment and, if the company fails, they will lose all of it. It is also not possible for investors to contemplate selling the purchased shares term; there is no established secondary market where investors can sell their shares in early-stage or private unlisted companies.

This has resulted in crowdfunding regulators setting restrictions on investments by non-accredited investors[2] and limiting the amount an individual investor can invest in crowdfunding offerings over a 12-month period. These restrictions are based on the (self-certified) individual investor's net worth and income (investments, usually, must represent no more than 10% of investors' liquid assets, although this varies across countries).

Due to the risks associated to equity investment, crowd equity-funding platforms conduct due diligence in relation to the companies that apply for funding, to ensure that the information provided about the company to investors is accurate and to avoid the risk of potential fraudulent behaviour. However, there are substantial differences in the implementation of due diligence procedures across countries in Europe (European Union, 2017).

A company/entrepreneur that launches an online fundraising equity campaign has between 30 and 60 days to achieve their target funding. At the end of the fundraising period, if the target amount has been reached (most equity crowdfunding platforms adopt an all-or-nothing funding approach), investors become company shareholders and are eligible for a return on their investment in the medium-long term, based on the value of the company.

5.1.1 Equity crowdfunding platforms in the UK: Crowdcube and Seedrs

Since the UK leads the European equity crowdfunding market, we look at this market in the UK in more detail, focusing specifically on the two most active equity crowdfunding platforms: Crowdcube and Seedrs.

Crowdcube was founded in 2011 by Darren Westlake and Luke Lang, and Seedrs was established in 2012 by Jeff Lynn and Carlos Silva. Both platforms are authorised and regulated by the UK Financial Conduct Authority (FCA) and are ranked respectively first and second in the UK equity crowdfunding market for volume of funding raised by companies and number of transactions (Ziegler et al., 2018). Crowdcube and Seedrs were the first online investment platforms to launch in the UK and have experienced massive growth since. Both platforms adopt an all-or-nothing funding approach, which means entrepreneurs receive the funding only if the campaign achieves 100% of the pre-set target amount (Belleflamme et al., 2010; Cumming et al., 2015; Haas et al., 2014). If the target amount is not achieved, the investors are repaid their money.

Platforms operate a transaction-fee business model, which means that companies are charged fees based on the amount transacted. Crowdcube imposes a fee of 7% for a successful pitch and Seedrs charges 7.5% on the funds raised. Other fees, such as management fees, for the provision of additional services are payable by the entrepreneur to the relevant platform, although, the platforms do not charge entrepreneurs for listing their businesses.

Start-up, early, and growth stage businesses, from a broad range of sectors, can try to raise finance on these platforms. The minimum target amount for fundraisers is £50,000 on Crowdcube. On average, during the past years, company have raised between £100,000 and £150,000 on Crowdcube. According to the Crowdcube website, the largest amount raised to date was for BrewDog, a Scottish craft beer maker, which raised £10 million to fund its US expansion plans. Seedrs has no minimum or maximum amounts. However, both of these platforms suggest that companies should avoid amounts that would result in a controlling share.

Once the enterprise has prepared are the necessary information on the business, it applies to the platform to launch its fundraising campaign. Both Crowdcube and Seedrs have dedicated teams that review the applications and perform due diligence to ensure that the information is "fair, clear, and not misleading." This ensures a minimum level of quality of the projects promoted and satisfies the Financial Conduct Authority requirements to protect small investors. The platforms' websites detail their due diligence procedures related to legal, financial, and compliance issues.

Once the project is approved, the campaign goes live on the platform for 30 to 60 days when investors can make bids to back the company. There is an overfunding period, which occurs if the target is achieved before the target time has expired; the enterprise then has the option to offer additional equity on the same terms.

Both of the platforms have been successful in helping businesses to raise capital. In 2017, Seedrs raised £84.2 million of investment on its platform and Crowdcube raised £95 million. Both platforms are internationalising, using different models. Crowdcube relies on local partners for its international expansion, while Seedrs runs its foreign investments from its UK platform, which ensures a unified structure and compliance with UK law.

Individual investors in Europe can invest in start-ups via these platforms. Following a registration process, investors are required to self-certify their understanding of the high-risk nature of investing in start-ups and early stage businesses, by completing what Seedrs calls its Investment Authorisation Questionnaire. An investor can invest between full amount sought by the business and £10; thus, it is possible to become a shareholder and acquire voting rights for a very small investment.

The possibility to become a company shareholder for small amounts of money is a crucial element of the success of equity crowdfunding. Equity crowdfunding investors in a successful campaign become fully-fledged shareholders, with rights to a return on their investment if the company performs well (Ahlers et al., 2015).

Although Crowdcube and Seedrs are similar in many respects, the diverge in how investors retain and control their shares.

Crowdcube allows entrepreneurs a dual class share structure, in which ordinary shares can be issued with or without voting rights and the investor holds shares in the funded company (see Figure 5.1).

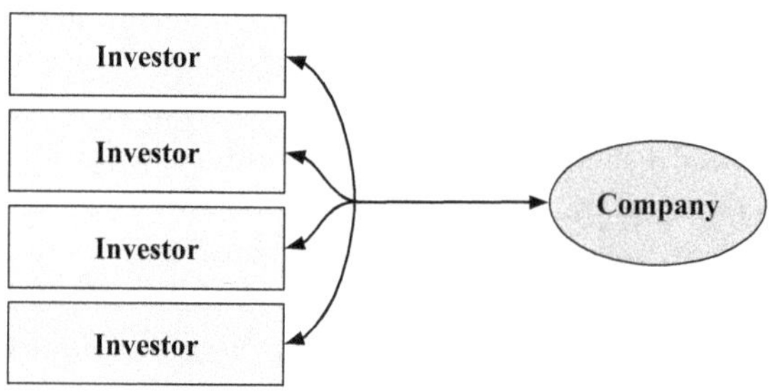

FIGURE 5.1 Crowdcube direct shareholdership structure

Companies can choose their capital structure and share types. Type A shareholders have pre-emption rights, and their numbers depend on the inclusion of a minimum investment threshold. Type A shareholders have full voting rights. Type B shareholders do not get pre-emption rights; they are at the discretion of the entrepreneur. Entrepreneurs can choose their preferred combination of share classes and investors are clear, at the time of their investment, about what they will receive.

Seedrs adopts a nominee approach to managing shareholders. A nominee arrangement gives the nominee legal title to the shares for the benefit of a third party (see Figure 5.2). In this case the nominee is the Seedrs platform, which is the legal shareholder in the relevant company's shareholder register and holds these shares on behalf of the various individuals who invest in the company. Full economic interest – including individual benefits from schemes, such as SEIS and EIS – are passed through to the underlying investors. All shares issued through Seedrs are voting shares.

Crowdcube has recently established itself as a company that can act as the nominee. However, the platform applies the nominee structure only to enterprises raising more than £250,000.

The advantage of the nominee structure for investors is the rapid distribution of share ownership and the possibility to outsource administration of their investments. The nominee, which is responsible for establishing the contractual rights in investment agreements with the funded business, ensures that investors' interests are protected. Investors retain the right (but are not obliged) to invest in the company's future fundraising rounds in order to maintain their share of the company equity; this is described as pre-emption rights.

For fundraisers, having a nominee is beneficial to avoid individual transactions with shareholders over administrative issues such as achieving consent and shareholder votes. Thus, companies seeking investors' agreement to strategic decisions liaise with Seedrs which, then, liaises with the individual investors. An additionaly benefit for fundraisers is the possibility to be more attractive to professional investors who might be interested in supporting the company in further funding rounds. Having a nominee that holds the crowd's shares and acts on behalf of the crowd of investors, makes the company more appealing for later stage professional investors, such as venture capitalists and private equity funds, who may be reluctant to invest

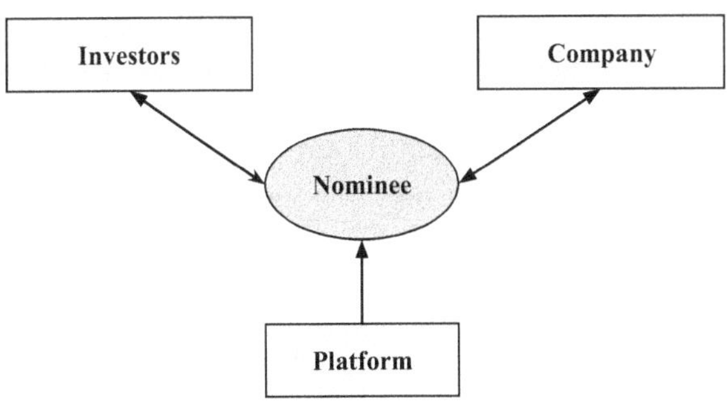

FIGURE 5.2 Seedrs nominee shareholdership structure

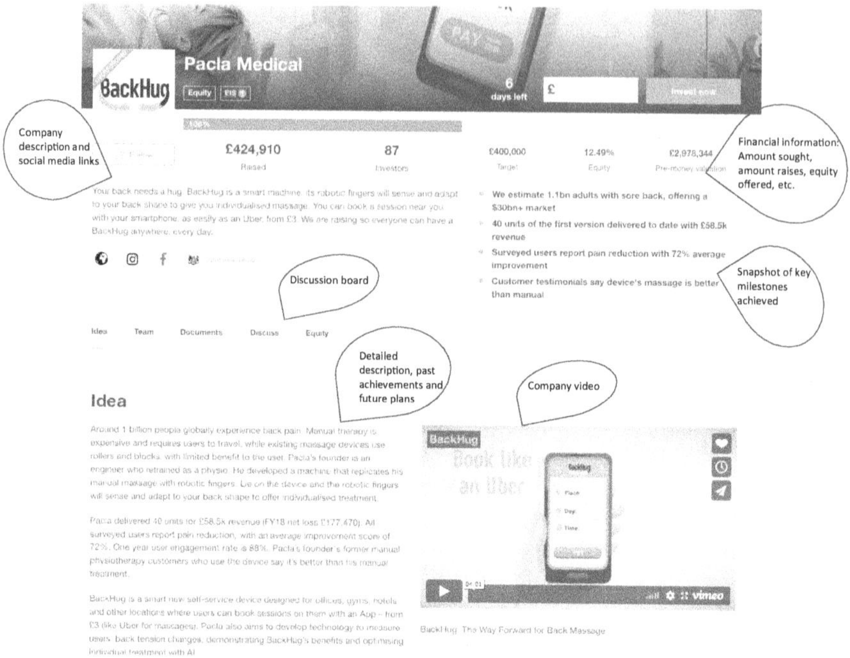

FIGURE 5.3 Pacla Medical equity crowdfunding campaign on Crowdcube

in a company with a widely scattered, worldwide shareholding base because of the time needed to obtain agreements to decisions (Butticè et al., 2019).

Figure 5.3 is an example of an equity crowdfunding campaign launched by Pacla Medical on Crowdcube.

The campaign's first page is the most important. It should provide a brief and effective description of the company including its social media links, financial information such as fundraising target (£400,000 in this case), percentage of equity offered to crowd investors (12.49%), pre-money company valuation, that is the calculated value of the company before receiving the next round of financing, and an update on fundraising status, that is the amount raised (£424,910 in this case) and numbers of investors (87 in this case).

Pacla Medical provided a snapshot of the main milestones achieved, in terms of market potential, number of products sold, partnerships with established companies, recognition from the press or existing users, etc. The aim was to signal to potential crowd investors the market validation received for the product on offer.

Uploading a video pitch is an important element of crowdfunding (Mollick, 2014). Most companies provide a video pitch lasting between 3 and 5 minutes where the company founders explain their product or service, their goals, and their achievements. The rest of the campaign provides a more detailed description of the idea or product, the market, company's past achievements and future plans. Equity crowdfunding campaigns typically include a section devoted to a description of the team and the founders, including a brief summary of their expertise, education, and a link to their LinkedIn profiles.

The platform offers a virtual space, a "discussion board," where potential investors can communicate with the entrepreneurs to obtain clarifications or more details on the company before making their investment decision. When the campaign closes, the discussion section can be used by the entrepreneur to communicate company updates and results to investors.

Table 5.1 presents the results of a qualitative study of some 600 equity crowdfunding campaign published via Seedrs and Crowdcube between April 2017 and March 2019. In view of the importance of signalling company quality

TABLE 5.1 Companies' achievements and future plans in equity crowdfunding campaign

Recurrent themes	*Categories*
Previous successful crowdfunding campaigns	Funding
Funds received from professional investors (VCs, Business Angel funding, etc.)	
Other (EU funds, government finance, etc.)	
Sales and users acquisition	Company tractions
Financial performance: revenues or profits	
Company awards	Media recognition
Media and newspaper coverage	
Existing collaboration with industry partners	Partnerships
Existing collaboration with clients/suppliers	
Founder's and team's industry experience	Founder experience
Founder's entrepreneurial experience (i.e. founder of previous companies)	
Patents, licences, IP rights	Technology ownership
Implementation of additional features to existing product	Product development
Portfolio development	
Market penetration: opening of new shops in the domestic market	Expansion strategy
Company international expansion	
Exit strategy via acquisition by market leaders/competitors or via IPO	Exit strategy
Future fundraising via crowdfunding	Future fundraising
Future fundraising via professional investors (VCs, Business Angels, etc.)	
Future fundraising via other entities (EU, government, etc.)	
Invitation to attend events and fairs	Events
Negotiation with industry partners to set up a collaboration	External connections
Planned new hires (CTO, MD, marketing director, etc.)	Team expansion
Revenues and users acquisition projections	Growth forecast

to attract potential investors (Ahlers et al., 2015; Kim and Viswanathan, 2019), our study provides examples of information related to companies' past achievements and future plans, which the entrepreneurs disclose to investors to signal company quality, reduce information asymmetries (Ahlers et al., 2015; Vismara, 2018), and achieve campaign fundraising success.

The most common themes related to past achievements refer to the company's fundraising track record, acquisition of new clients, partnerships with established companies in the industry, and external recognition from the press or other media. Entrepreneurs also provide information on IP rights to the technology used, past experience of company development, and past experience in the industry. Entrepreneurs provide information on activities planned to further develop the business: related to development or finalisation of a product, company expansion strategy (local and global), negotiations with established firms in the market to establish potential collaborations, team expansion, and financial projections. Entrepreneurs also provide information to potential investors on their exit strategy – i.e. opportunities for investors to liquidate their investment, and mention external recognition in the form of invitations to participate in important events in their field.

5.2 Why do entrepreneurs use equity crowdfunding?

Chapters 2 and 3 showed that crowdfunding is an important way for young entrepreneurs to access seed funds. Specifically, equity crowdfunding, involving the exchange of company share to individual investors in exchange of small contribution, enlarges the sources of financing available to entrepreneurs, such as family and friends or angel investors, and often is the first source of funding sought by the entrepreneur. Due to the important part played by equity crowdfunding in boosting the entrepreneurial ecosystem across countries (Ziegler et al., 2019), it is important to understand what drives crowd fundraising and, more specifically, how entrepreneurs benefit from crowdfunding.

The qualitative research that forms part of this book was aimed at understanding what drives entrepreneurs to use equity crowdfunding initially and the advantages it provides beyond financial capital. The sample includes 25 European start-ups that used equity crowdfunding between 2013 and 2014 whose founders were interviewed. These start-ups come from different industries and countries and are at different stages of development (see Figure 5.4).

The average amount raised by our respondents on equity crowdfunding platforms was £267,000 from an average of 174 investors. We identified five different drivers of crowdfunding: (i) fundraising speed; (ii) testing existence of a market for the business idea and advertising the idea; (iii) attracting investments from professional investors; (iv) retaining control of the company; and (v) obtaining the support of passionate investors.

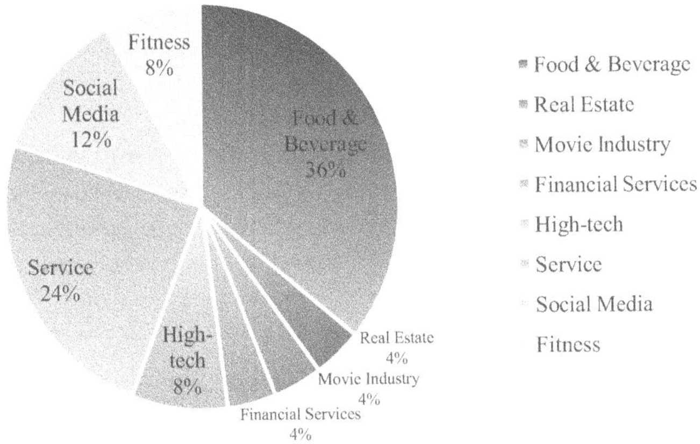

FIGURE 5.4 Sample companies' industry

5.2.1 Speed of fundraising

Crowdfunding is an important financial tool for entrepreneurs who may not have access to other sources of finance. Companies in the very early stages of development, when the product is not ready for commercialisation and the company has no revenue stream, can find it difficult to attract traditional professional investors. In this case, crowdfunding is a way for entrepreneurs to obtain financing for their companies.

One interviewee told us that:

> Venture capitalists usually provide growth funding and not early stage funding. You really need to prove your business is able to grow ten times before professional investors get interested in your company, so for us the crowd was the best passage. Also, professional investors usually want you to have launched the product and have performance traction about people using your product, revenues, etc. Company A, Founder.

The interviewees reported that one of their main concerns was to raise money quickly to enable development of the product or marketing strategy. So speed is important. Fundraising from professional investors can be lengthy and time consuming (Van Osnabrugge, 2000), whereas crowdfunding allows the finance to be raised in 30–60 days. There is a clear deadline set for the fundraising effort. One interview reported:

> I thought one of the positive aspects of crowdfunding is that it gives you a clear deadline. With angel investors very often you don't get yes or no when you ask for funding, you get "keep me in the loop." Much better is when they tell you that you have three months for reaching your target amount, after that you either fail or you get it. Company B, Founder

Also, crowdfunding allows the entrepreneur to raise just enough money to achieve the next milestone. Just enough money allows development of the business to demonstrate its value and attract further investors. As reported by one interviewee:

> It was the first time I had tried to raise investment for my new company. We thought we would start off by raising a small amount so that I could hire a sales person and have money to spend on marketing. I wanted to raise a small amount of capital just to prove the concept of my business and to show that we could have a crowd of people backing the idea. Company C, Founder

5.2.2 Test the market and obtain public exposure

In addition to obtaining financing, crowdfunding allows the entrepreneur to test the market for the business idea and advertise it. Entrepreneurial firms exploit opportunities to bring new products and services to market. A successful business idea is critical to the new venture's success. The entrepreneur must be ready to exploit circumstances favourable to the creation and launch of a new product, service, or business (Hayton et al., 2011), and follow this up by testing its feasibility (Barringer, 2015). Feasibility analysis involves determining whether a business idea is viable and worth pursuing. The objective is to establish whether there is market demand for the product. Feasibility analysis involves discussion with industry experts, surveying prospective customers, studying industry trends, etc. Potential customers can overestimate their intent to purchase a product or service and the results of customer surveys must be interpreted with some caution.

Crowdfunding is seen as an opportunity to validate the business idea, create and assess the customer community prior to commercialisation. Crowdfunding allows the entrepreneur to understand the market potential of the product or service and create a loyal community in a short space of time, which is something that can take years for those seeking funding from traditional financial sources. Willingness to invest in the business can be understood as the business idea having potential value.

Most of our respondents said the main reason for using equity crowdfunding was the possibility to validate the business concept before starting to invest in its development, thus, the main reason was marketing. One entrepreneur told us that:

> I approached crowdfunding to establish a customer base before commercialising the product. It was purely a marketing exercise as opposed to financial raising measure. You are establishing the foundations of the business before actually you go to any large expense; it means that the likelihood of success of the business is much more. With crowdfunding you can figure out very quickly if the market approves of your product. And if you can be successful in your finance raise, your business becomes a very well-known story and you can raise a community and establish what most businesses do over ten years from day one. Company D, founder.

Other entrepreneurs reinforced the importance of using crowdfunding to test the market before investing large amount of resources in manufacturing the product:

> One of the biggest risks with bringing a product to market is the manufacturing cost. Crowdfunding reduces these risks, because if the campaign fails, we don't have to waste money trying to build something that nobody wants. The best way to test if someone is willing to pay for it, is to ask them to pay for it. Company E, co-founder.

Finally, crowdfunding provides validation of the idea from a large crowd of people, which is better than relying on the judgment of two or three investors, who may not be interested in supporting the project further:

> The reason we went crowdfunding is because we needed something to validate the product. If you have one investor who put 100,000 euros, that is not necessary a validation of the product, but when you have 180 investors, that is a good validation. That means that there is a demand for that product, people liked it. Company F, founder.

Overall, it seems that crowdfunding represents an opportunity for the entrepreneur to assess the market potential of the product or service, advertise it, and create a community of customers before commercialisation. Crowdfunding is used to legitimise the business idea.

Previous works emphasises the importance of legitimacy for acquiring critical initial resources to allow a sustainable organisation (Stinchcombe, 1965). New ventures tend to lack legitimacy and, especially, if they are in nascent sectors with no established organisational forms or categories. Lack of legitimacy can be problematic for entrepreneurs seeking funding. Crowdfunding provides an opportunity to build legitimacy to the minimum threshold necessary to attract external resource providers (Zimmerman and Zeitz, 2002). Also, validating the business concept via crowdfunding and demonstrating the existence of a market reduces information asymmetries between the entrepreneur and subsequent investors. It provides professional investors with more means of estimating the value of the venture (Chua et al., 2011; Elitzur and Gavious, 2003; Sapienza and Korsgaard, 1996).

5.2.3 Attract investments from professional investors

It can be difficult to attract financial partners in the early stages of business development (Berger and Udell, 1998). However, business angels and venture capitalists are among the most important equity owners in the start-up phase (George et al., 2005). Entrepreneurs often seek additional funds after a successful crowdfunding campaign to allow the development and improvement of their product. However, the selection processes of venture capitalists and business angels is strict and only companies able to demonstrate high growth potential will be successful (Baum and Silverman, 2004; Bertoni et al., 2015; Puri and Zarutskie, 2012). Professional investors tend to become involved in the later stages of company development, when the product or service has been commercialised and its value demonstrated. Thus, equity crowdfunding is important for raising the initial funding required to kick start a business (Walthoff-Borm et al., 2018a) and demonstrate value. It can act as a positive signal of the quality and value of the business to later potential investors (Kuppuswammy and Roth, 2016). One respondent told us that:

> We raised £360,000 on Seedrs, then we got £125,000 from an investment fund, and then £50,000 from an Argentinian private investor. It is not likely these investors would have invested if we weren't fully funded in equity crowdfunding, because professional investors do not like to go into a business too early, so they just hang around and wait. Crowdfunding helped us in this sense. Company G, founder.

The founder of a fitness activities company in London was successful in a crowdfunding round, which persuaded professional investors to invest in the company. She reported:

> We are trying to raise money through venture capitalists, they liked the fact that we had a successful crowdfunding campaign, because they see that you persuaded people to invest in your company. They read the comments; they see something about you. If you just approach them out of the blue, they have nothing to read about you and they are not willing to invest. Company H, founder

Successful equity crowdfunding helped endows credibility and reduces information asymmetries (Roma et al., 2017; Colombo and Shafi, 2016; Vismara, 2018). Incomplete or scarce information increases the risk of poor judgement of the new venture's potential and, thus, is a barrier to obtaining capital from equity or debt markets (Baum and Silverman, 2004; Ahlers et al., 2015; Vismara, 2018).

5.2.4 Retain company control

Many entrepreneurs reported that they preferred crowdfunding because it allowed them to retain control of the company and avoided investors interfering in their strategic planning and goals (Hellmann, 1998). Professional funding can channel the company into success being defined by value creation (Hellmann, 1998). Rapid growth can overshadow other objectives. Entrepreneurs want to protect their private benefits and values whereas venture capitalists want to maximise their financial returns (Gertner et al., 1994; Hannan et al., 1996).

Professional investors' objectives of good and quick financial returns from their investments may not match the entrepreneur's business vision:

> We approached equity crowdfunding because we heard quite few hard stories about professional investors chasing you for reports, results, and building billion dollars business very quickly. I think we wanted to avoid that from happening. We left our corporate job to work for ourselves and we didn't really feel comfortable with the idea of having someone involved in our business who is only really involved to make money out of us. Company I, co-founder.

Also, a London gourmet pizza business rejected an investment offer from a venture capitalist fund to avoid losing control of the company. The entrepreneur reported:

> We started to negotiate from a pool of private investors. They created a syndicate of investors and they wanted to invest all the money we were raising by themselves. After a couple of months, they contacted me to make an offer. They said: instead of 40% of the company, we want 65% of the company shares. I turned down their offer. In the meantime, I was negotiating with a Private Equity fund. At the end they also wanted 65% of the company shares. All of them wanted to have the control, but since it is my company and it was my idea, I want to be able to manage and develop it in the way I think is more appropriate. Company L, founder.

Overall, our research shows that many entrepreneurs are reluctant to seek professional investor support in the early stages of their business. The decision to use crowdfunding does not necessarily preclude participation of other investors; it is a strategic choice. Our interviewees took the view that there are other sources of investment apart from venture capital funding. Crowdfunding represents an alternative that facilitates development of their business ideas in accordance with their initial plans.

5.2.5 Receive support from passionate investors

Another reason for preferring crowdfunding is the benefit derived from the formation of a community of people who believe in the business and are willing to support its further development. As the founder of a company that rents desk space in the UK, explained:

> Most VCs think that they have smart money and that they add a lot of value. I believe that the crowd adds just as much value. I think that having the crowd is more democratic than having a couple of opinions. I think that having a crowd makes more sense. Company L, founder.

There are advantages, also, of investors with different perspectives which can promote business growth. The same interviewee told us that:

> Through crowdfunding you attract people who believe in what you are doing, they are not only investing for returns, they believe in the business and they are passionate. VCs are good but they wouldn't have the enthusiasm for the business that would allow growing and learning. People who are enthusiastic tend to see things differently, they tend to spot opportunities, and to see problems that you wouldn't notice. Company L, founder.

It seems that entrepreneurs use crowdfunding for various strategic and financial reasons. In the next sub-section, we summarise the advantages of crowdfunding.

5.3 Strategic and financial benefits of equity crowdfunding

Drawing on entrepreneurs' experience of equity crowdfunding, we found that crowdfunding is more than a financial tool. Table 5.2 presents the main strategic and financial benefits entrepreneurs obtain from using equity crowdfunding.

The strategic benefits of crowdfunding include the entrepreneur's ability to manage the uncertainty characterising new business development. Crowdfunding allows the entrepreneur to validate the business concept by proving that a market exists for the product and to build a community of people interested in and willing to buy the product prior to commercialisation. It represents an opportunity for the entrepreneur to achieve public exposure and to obtain feedback on product/service, which contributes to the fine-tuning of the project (Belleflamme et al., 2013; Gerber et al., 2012).

TABLE 5.2 The benefits of equity crowdfunding for entrepreneurs

Strategic benefits		*Financial benefits*	
Product validation Market validation Creation of a customer-base	Product and market testing	Quick fundraising Small amounts Filling financial gap	Kick-start funding
Public exposure Marketing channel for the business	Marketing	Quality signal for stakeholders and investors	Attracting further finance
Retaining control of the company Company valuation decision	Governance		
Support from passionate people Leverage of crowd knowledge	Creating a community		

Crowdfunding is also a marketing tool (Mollick and Kuppuswamy, 2014); it exposes the business to the public and allows the potential product to be "advertised." Another advantage of crowdfunding is that it allows the entrepreneur to retain control over the business (Gerber et al., 2012) while demonstrating to more traditional financers that there is demand for the product/service (Mollick, 2014). It allows the entrepreneur to continue to make strategic decisions in line with the original idea.

Crowdfunding provides the organisation with legitimacy and proof of business quality and existence of a solid customer-base. Legitimacy is a conferred quality, which is under the control of individuals external to the firm (Pfeffer and Salancik, 1978).

The financial benefits of crowdfunding include the entrepreneur's ability to raise small amounts of funds necessary to kick-start their business as well as attract stakeholders and professional investors with substantial resources (Stinchcombe, 1965; Zimmerman and Zeitz, 2002). The higher likelihood of failure for young organisations is due primarily to external factors such as low level of legitimacy and inability to forge links with key environmental constituencies (Singh et al., 1986).

By demonstrating the crowd's enthusiasm for the business idea, based on their willingness to invest in it, entrepreneurs are able to attract subsequent funding from more traditional investors, such as venture capitalists and business angels, who, otherwise, might have been reluctant to invest. Thus, increases organisation legitimacy, favouring resource transfer (Dowling and Pfeffer, 1975) based on endorsement by a collective of early-stage investors (see Figure 5.5).

We can conclude that successful crowdfunding can signal quality and allow investors to judge the firm's potential, which helps to reduce information asymmetry. The literature suggests that information asymmetry is a major problem for entrepreneurs and reduces the ability of potential investors to estimate project legitimacy (Elitzur and Gavious, 2003; Sapienza and Korsgaard, 1996; Baum and Silverman, 2004; Ahlers et al., 2015; Vismara, 2018).

FIGURE 5.5 Company legitimation via crowdfunding

5.4 Risks related to equity crowdfunding

Equity crowdfunding adds to the democratisation of finance by allowing small and medium-sized investors to purchase shares in new companies. Section 5.1 shows that crowdfunding gives access to investment opportunities, for individuals with small amounts of money to invest in business ideas. It reduces the search costs for non-professional investors, who benefit, also, from the due diligence and risk assessment that the platforms carry out. Equity crowdfunding allows individuals to support start-ups, products, services, brands, and ideas which they are enthusiastic about.

Section 5.3 highlighted the financial and strategic advantages of crowdfunding for entrepreneurs. Equity crowdfunding enables start-ups to obtain capital via individual online contributions, to test the product market, to create a community of people, and to advertise their business. However, investing in an early-stage business carries some level of risk for the actors involved. Below, we discuss the risks related to investing and raising funds via equity crowdfunding, from the points of view of the investor, the entrepreneur, and the platform.

5.4.1 Entrepreneur risks

Despite the strategic and financial benefits of equity crowdfunding, there are some potential downsides for entrepreneurs. Choice of the platform is the first issue: selecting the most appropriate platform requires analysis, for instance, of the platforms' rules concerning the percentage retained by the platform of the amount raised, fees related to the due diligence process, performance indicators such as fundraising success rates, average amounts invested, length of time investing is possible, and the characteristics of investors that the platform attracts (Dushnitsky and Fitza, 2018).

Furthermore, although compliance with the platform's procedures is relatively quick, preparing the pitch and meeting the due diligence requirements imposed by the platform require some preparation before presentation to the public. Entrepreneurs need to consider the costs and time related to the (video) pitch, updates, and day-to-day management of the campaign, including responding to investors' questions and providing feedback via the platform, as well as the post-investment activities related to updating investors, the legal and administrative processes related to share issuance, etc.

The public nature of crowdfunding can be a deterrent to entrepreneurs fearful of information disclosure to potential competitors who may not be genuine investors. For instance, one interviewee who had used equity crowdfunding in the UK told us that:

> The difficult thing about crowdfunding is that you have to put your business plan out in a very public arena, everybody can read your business plan including your competitors and people can comment on it, on your approach, or on you personally on a public accessible website, hiding behind a username. So you don't know whether they are potentially big investors or somebody who is you competitor and wants you to fail. Company K, founder.

Crowdfunding entails intellectual property risks, which the entrepreneur must consider before launching the campaign. For instance, if the crowdfunding platform requires specific technical details (e.g. related to electronic devices) whose secrecy is needed to maintain competitive advantage, this might result in the invention no longer being patentable. The entrepreneur must be aware of patentability issues and, perhaps, submit a patent application before the campaign goes live.

Finally, entrepreneurs who use crowdfunding are exposed to the risk of public failure, which could undermine the company's reputation and ability to attract funding from other sources or attract partners to develop the business.

5.4.2 Investor risks

Despite the advantages of democratisation of finance, investing in early stage companies via crowdfunding carries several risks related to the investors' expertise, asymmetric information, financing stage, decision-making process, market illiquidity, and moral hazard.

Typically, crowdfunding campaigns involve large numbers of amateur investors, who invest small amounts of money in early-stage businesses. These small investors may lack expertise in evaluating the start-up. Hence, their investment decisions may not be validated, but rather driven by personal knowledge, passion and interest, geographical proximity, and peer influence (Agrawal et al., 2011, 2015; Lee and Lee, 2012; Zhang and Liu, 2012).

Although information asymmetry is a concern for both professional and crowd investors (Cumming and Johan, 2013; Ley and Weaven, 2011; Ahlers et al., 2015; Vismara, 2018), the former have more tools and processes available to access information about the business. For example, professional investors are able to conduct extensive due diligence via frequent meetings with firm founders, collect independent references, perform a detailed financial analysis, and demand for comprehensive business plans (Jensen, 1993; Sahlman, 1990). In this case, the investment process takes a considerable time (Van Osnabrugge, 2000). Crowdfunding investors have limited information and limited time to assess the business (online campaigns last 60 days, on average), entrepreneurs may be reluctant to disclose sensitive information online, and crowdfunding investors rarely have an opportunity to meet the firm's founders (Di Pietro et al., 2018). Mollick (2014) suggests that investors face information flow risks since there are no statutory requirements for unlisted companies to disclose any changes to how the business is run or its operational activities. Thus, checking firm performance can be difficult for these small shareholders, who have to rely on the information provided by the entrepreneur which might be overoptimistic (Shane and Cable, 2002; Shane and Stuart, 2002; Cooper et al., 1988; Busenitz and Barney, 1997; Baron, 1998).

Investors face risks related to the intrinsic nature of early stage investments. In contrast to more mature businesses with performance track records, early-stage ventures rely on the development of a new product or service for which the market may be unknown (Brush et al., 2001). This makes crowdfunding investments more speculative than later-stage investments which tend to involve professional investors.

Due to the limited information available, crowdfunding investors may follow the "herd" or the latest trend (Zhang and Liu, 2012) in the absence of any due diligence process; this is described as "investment path dependency" (Agrawal et al., 2011; European Commission, 2015; Kirby and Worner, 2014; Scharfstein and Stein, 1990).

Market illiquidity is another investor risk. The lack of a secondary market for equity crowdfunding shares, such as a virtual space to exchange or sell the shares, means that the only realisable gain relies on dividends or the sale of the company. The exit opportunities for crowdfunders are restricted (Hornuf and Schwienbacher, 2016). Dilution is an additional risk: most start-ups raise more funding later in the development process, which can "dilute" the crowdfund investors' influence on the company and the potential returns on their investment.

Lastly, moral hazard refers to the inability of the crowdfund investor to rely on a contractual agreement with the venture to reduce the changes of opportunistic behaviour by the entrepreneur after receipt of the funding (Belleflamme et al., 2014; Hornuf and Schwienbacher, 2016). Crowdfunding contracts tend to be very simple since the individual stakes typically are lower and the relationship tend to be based more on online trust than contractual clauses.

For all these reasons, investing via crowdfunding involves gambling on the ability of the entrepreneurs to achieve an outcome.

5.4.3 Platform risk

Crowdfunding platforms create value by facilitating exchanges of resources (financial and non-financial) between two main actors: investors, which represent the supply side of the platform, and companies, which represent the demand side. The platform benefits from the participation of large numbers of customers and to facilitate the exchanges, the platform must create large, scalable, and accessible networks of entrepreneurs and investors. The platform retains a fee based on a percentage of the amount raised in a successful campaign. A larger number of start-ups and investors connected by the platform, enhances platform reputation in the market and increases the probability it will be exploited by others. A sign of platform quality is campaign success rates, that is, the number of successful fundraising campaigns relative to the number of the campaigns hosted by the platforms. Other important metrics include total amount transacted via the platform, average length (time) of the campaign, average number of investors, and average amounts invested. These attributes are used by potential users to evaluate platform quality.

Managing a crowdfunding platform carries some risk. Unclear regulation and tax laws can influence the crowdfunding activity. Equity crowdfunding platforms are responsible for conducting due diligence and verification tests and checks on the companies, to appraise their quality and increase the chances of a successful

TABLE 5.3 Risks of equity crowdfunding for entrepreneurs, investors, and platforms

	Risks of equity crowdfunding
ENTREPRENEURS	• Business-platform fit • Time-demanding • Information disclosure • IPR protection • Risk of public failure
INVESTORS	• Lack of expertise to evaluate investments • Information asymmetries • Uncertain payoffs linked to early-stage finance • Entrepreneur optimism about prospective performance • Weak disclosure obligations for start-up • Market illiquidity – absence of a secondary market • Risk of dilution • Moral hazard
PLATFORMS	• Ambiguous regulatory environment • Scrupulous scrutiny to assess business quality • Fundraising failure may signal low scrutiny capacity • Post-funding businesses performance

fundraising. Fundraising failure can be a signal of low levels of scrutiny by the platform operator, which might reduce the chances of entrepreneurs using that platform. Lastly, the reputation of the equity crowdfunding platform is linked, also, to business performance after the campaign, which includes business survival rates, subsequent funds raised from professional investors, firm growth, and expansion, etc.

Crowdfunding, similar to all investment opportunities, carries some level of risk. See Table 5.3 for a summary of the risks and the actors affected.

Note that many of these risks are not confined to equity crowdfunding. Some apply to other forms of crowdfunding such as reward-based crowdfunding and P2P lending crowdfunding (see Section 2.3 for a description of different crowdfunding types).

Notes

1 See for more information: https://www.seis.co.uk/; https://www.gov.uk/guidance/venture-capital-schemes-apply-for-the-enterprise-investment-scheme

2 In the US, a non-accredited investor is any investor who does not meet the income or net worth requirements set out by the Securities and Exchange Commission (SEC): one who has a net worth of less than $1 million (including spouse) and who earned less than $200,000 annually ($300,000 with spouse) in the previous two years. In the EU, and in the UK, an non-accredited investor has a net worth of less than €1 million and has not participated as investor in funds for more than €50,000.

See for more information: https://www.investor.gov/additional-resources/news-alerts/alerts-bulletins/updated-investor-bulletin-accredited-investors; https://www.prospectus.com/private-placement-memorandum-services-information/experienced-investors/

References

Agrawal, A., Catalini, C. and Goldfarb, A., 2015. Crowdfunding: Geography, social networks, and the timing of investment decisions. *Journal of Economics & Management Strategy, 24*(2), 253–274.

Agrawal, A.K., Catalini, C. and Goldfarb, A., 2011. *The Geography of Crowdfunding (No. w16820)*. National Bureau of Economic Research, Cambridge, MA.

Ahlers, G.K., Cumming, D., Günther, C. and Schweizer, D., 2015. Signaling in equity crowdfunding. *Entrepreneurship Theory and Practice, 39*(4), pp. 955–980.

Baron, R.A., 1998. Cognitive mechanisms in entrepreneurship: Why and when entrepreneurs think differently than other people. *Journal of Business Venturing, 13*(4), pp. 275–294.

Barringer, B.R., 2015. *Entrepreneurship: Successfully Launching New Ventures*. Pearson Education India, Upper Saddle River, NJ.

Baum, J.A. and Silverman, B.S., 2004. Picking winners or building them? Alliance, intellectual, and human capital as selection criteria in venture financing and performance of biotechnology startups. *Journal of Business Venturing, 19*(3), pp. 411–436.

Belleflamme, P., Lambert, T. and Schwienbacher, A., 2010. Crowdfunding: An industrial organization perspective. In *Prepared for the Workshop Digital Business Models: Understanding Strategies'*, June, Paris, France (pp. 25–26).

Belleflamme, P., Lambert, T. and Schwienbacher, A., 2013. Individual crowdfunding practices. *Venture Capital, 15*(4), pp. 313–333.

Belleflamme, P., Lambert, T. and Schwienbacher, A., 2014. Crowdfunding: Tapping the right crowd. *Journal of Business Venturing, 29*(5), pp. 585–609.

Berger, A.N. and Udell, G.F., 1998. The economics of small business finance: The roles of private equity and debt markets in the financial growth cycle. *Journal of Banking & Finance, 22*(6–8), pp. 613–673.

Bertoni, F., Colombo, M.G. and Quas, A., 2015. The patterns of venture capital investment in Europe. *Small Business Economics, 45*(3), pp. 543–560.

Brush, C.G., Greene, P.G. and Hart, M.M., 2001. From initial idea to unique advantage: The entrepreneurial challenge of constructing a resource base. *Academy of Management Perspectives, 15*(1), pp. 64–78.

Busenitz, L.W. and Barney, J.B., 1997. Differences between entrepreneurs and managers in large organizations: Biases and heuristics in strategic decision-making. *Journal of Business Venturing, 12*(1), pp. 9–30.

Butticè, V., Di Pietro, F. and Tenca, F., 2019. Is equity crowdfunding always good? The role of deal structure in influencing entrepreneurs' ability to attract professional investors. *Working paper presented at the 4th Entrepreneurial Conference*, Trier, Germany.

Chua, J.H., Chrisman, J.J., Kellermanns, F. and Wu, Z., 2011. Family involvement and new venture debt financing. *Journal of Business Venturing, 26*(4), pp. 472–488.

Colombo, M.G. and Shafi, K., 2016. Initial trust and the collaborations between new ventures and corporate venture capitals. In *Academy of Management Proceedings* (Vol. 2016, No. 1, p. 14152). Academy of Management, Briarcliff Manor, NY.

Cooper, A.C., Woo, C.Y. and Dunkelberg, W.C., 1988. Entrepreneurs' perceived chances for success. *Journal of Business Venturing, 3*(2), pp. 97–108.

Cumming, D.J. and Johan, S.A., 2013. *Venture Capital and Private Equity Contracting: An International Perspective*. Academic Press, Amsterdam, the Netherlands.

Cumming, D.J., Leboeuf, G. and Schwienbacher, A., 2015. Crowdfunding models: Keep-it-all vs. all-or-nothing. *Financial Management, 44*, pp. 1–30.

Cumming, D.J., Meoli, M. and Vismara, S., 2016. Corporate governance in equity crowdfunding. University of Bergamo working paper.

Di Pietro, F., Prencipe, A. and Majchrzak, A., 2018. Crowd equity investors: An underutilized asset for open innovation in startups. *California Management Review, 60*(2), pp. 43–70.

Dowling, J. and Pfeffer, J., 1975. Organizational legitimacy: Social values and organizational behavior. *Pacific Sociological Review, 18*(1), pp. 122–136.

Dushnitsky, G. and Fitza, M.A., 2018. Are we missing the platforms for the crowd? Comparing investment drivers across multiple crowdfunding platforms. *Journal of Business Venturing Insights, 10*, p. e00100.

Elitzur, R. and Gavious, A., 2003. Contracting, signaling, and moral hazard: A model of entrepreneurs, "angels," and venture capitalists. *Journal of Business Venturing, 18*(6), pp. 709–725.

European Commission, 2015. *Crowdfunding from an Investor Perspective*. European Commission, Brussels.

European Union, 2017. Identifying market and regulatory obstacles to cross border development of crowdfunding in the EU. Available at https://ec.europa.eu/info/sites/info/files/171216-crowdfunding-report_en.pdf.

George, G., Wiklund, J. and Zahra, S.A., 2005. Ownership and the internationalization of small firms. *Journal of Management, 31*(2), pp. 210–233.

Gerber, E.M., Hui, J.S. and Kuo, P.Y., 2012, February. Crowdfunding: Why people are motivated to post and fund projects on crowdfunding platforms. In *Proceedings of the International Workshop on Design, Influence, and Social Technologies: Techniques, Impacts and Ethics* (Vol. 2, No. 11, p. 10). Northwestern University, Evanston, IL.

Gertner, R.H., Scharfstein, D.S. and Stein, J.C., 1994. Internal versus external capital markets. *The Quarterly Journal of Economics, 109*(4), pp. 1211–1230.

Haas, P., Blohm, I. and Leimeister, J.M., 2014. An empirical taxonomy of crowdfunding intermediaries. *Thirty Fifth International Conference on Information Systems*, Auckland.

Hannan, M.T., Burton, M.D. and Baron, J.N., 1996. Inertia and change in the early years: Employment relations in young, high technology firms. *Industrial and Corporate Change, 5*(2), pp. 503–536.

Hayton, J., Chandler, G.N. and DeTienne, D.R., 2011. Entrepreneurial opportunity identification and new firm development processes: A comparison of family and non-family new ventures. *International Journal of Entrepreneurship and Innovation Management, 13*(1), pp. 12–31.

Hellmann, T., 1998. The allocation of control rights in venture capital contracts. *The Rand Journal of Economics, 29*, pp. 57–76.

Hornuf, L. and Schwienbacher, A., 2016. 15 Crowdinvesting: Angel investing for the masses? In C. Mason and H. Landström (eds.), *Handbook of Research on Business Angels* (p. 381). Edward Elgar Publishing.

Jensen, M.C., 1993. The modern industrial revolution, exit, and the failure of internal control systems. *The Journal of Finance, 48*(3), pp. 831–880.

Kim, K. and Viswanathan, S., 2019. The experts in the crowd: The role of experienced investors in a crowdfunding market. *MIS Quarterly, 43*(2), pp. 347–372.

Kirby, E. and Worner, S., 2014. Crowd-funding: An infant industry growing fast. Working paper, IOSCO Research Department.

Kuppuswammy, V. and Roth, K., 2016. *Research on the Current State of Crowdfunding: The Effect of Crowdfunding Performance and Outside Capital*. US Small Business Administration-Office of Advocacy, Washington, DC.

Lee, E. and Lee, B., 2012. Herding behavior in online P2P lending: An empirical investigation. *Electronic Commerce Research and Applications, 11*(5), pp. 495–503.

Ley, A. and Weaven, S., 2011. Exploring the agency dynamics of crowdfunding in start-up capital financing. *Academy of Entrepreneurship Journal*, *17*(1), pp. 85–111.

Mollick, E., 2014. The dynamics of crowdfunding: An exploratory study. *Journal of Business Venturing*, *29*(1), pp. 1–16.

Mollick, E.R. and Kuppuswamy, V., 2014. After the campaign: Outcomes of crowdfunding. UNC Kenan-Flagler Research Paper.

Pfeffer, J. and Salancik, G., 1978. *The External Control of Organizations: A Resource Dependence Approach*. Harper and Row Publishers, New York.

Puri, M. and Zarutskie, R., 2012. On the life cycle dynamics of venture-capital-and non-venture-capital-financed firms. *The Journal of Finance*, *67*(6), pp. 2247–2293.

Roma, P., Petruzzelli, A.M. and Perrone, G., 2017. From the crowd to the market: The role of reward-based crowdfunding performance in attracting professional investors. *Research Policy*, *46*(9), pp. 1606–1628.

Sahlman, W.A., 1990. The structure and governance of venture-capital organizations. *Journal of Financial Economics*, *27*(2), pp. 473–521.

Sapienza, H.J. and Korsgaard, M.A., 1996. Procedural justice in entrepreneur-investor relations. *Academy of Management Journal*, *39*(3), pp. 544–574.

Scharfstein, D.S. and Stein, J.C., 1990. Herd behavior and investment. *The American Economic Review*, *80*(3), pp. 465–479.

Shane, S. and Cable, D., 2002. Network ties, reputation, and the financing of new ventures. *Management Science*, *48*(3), pp. 364–381.

Shane, S. and Stuart, T., 2002. Organizational endowments and the performance of university start-ups. *Management Science*, *48*(1), pp. 154–170.

Singh, J.V., Tucker, D.J. and House, R.J., 1986. Organizational legitimacy and the liability of newness. *Administrative Science Quarterly*, pp. 171–193.

Stinchcombe, A.L., 1965. Organizations and social structure. *Handbook of Organizations*, *44*(2), pp. 142–193.

Van Osnabrugge, M., 2000. A comparison of business angel and venture capitalist investment procedures: An agency theory-based analysis. *Venture Capital: An International Journal of Entrepreneurial Finance*, *2*(2), pp. 91–109.

Vismara, S., 2018. Information cascades among investors in equity crowdfunding. *Entrepreneurship Theory and Practice*, *42*(3), pp. 467–497.

Walthoff-Borm, X., Schwienbacher, A. and Vanacker, T., 2018a. Equity crowdfunding: First resort or last resort? *Journal of Business Venturing*, *33*(4), pp. 513–533.

Walthoff-Borm, X., Vanacker, T.R. and Collewaert, V., 2018b. Equity crowdfunding, shareholder structures, and firm performance. *Corporate Governance: An International Review*, *26*(5), pp. 314–330.

Zhang, J. and Liu, P., 2012. Rational herding in microloan markets. *Management Science*, *58*(5), pp. 892–912.

Ziegler, T., Shneor, R., Garvey, K., Wenzlaff, K., Yerolemou, N., Hao, R. and Zhang, B., 2018. *Expanding Horizons: The 3rd European Alternative Finance Industry Report*. University of Cambridge, Cambridge Centre for Alternative Finance.

Ziegler, T., Shneor, R., Wenzlaff, K., Odorović, A., Johanson, D., Hao, R. and Ryll, L., 2019. *4th European Alternative Finance Benchmarking Report*. University of Cambridge, Cambridge Centre for Alternative Finance.

Zimmerman, M.A. and Zeitz, G.J., 2002. Beyond survival: Achieving new venture growth by building legitimacy. *Academy of Management Review*, *27*(3), pp. 414–431.

6

EQUITY CROWDFUNDING AS A STRATEGIC TOOL

The potential benefits of a long-lasting relationship between equity crowd investors and entrepreneurs are the main feature distinguishing equity crowdfunding from other crowdfunding models.

In this chapter, we look at the post-funding phase and explore how entrepreneurs can exploit the relationship with crowd investors to build competitive advantage. Following an overview of the state-of-the-art literature on equity crowdfunding, this chapter examines the benefits, in terms of knowledge and networks, that crowd investors provide to funded companies.

6.1 Review of the literature on equity crowdfunding

In 2017, in Europe, equity crowdfunding – a method of financing in which funds are provided in exchange for company shares – reached a significant level in terms of investment amounts. More than €200 million transactions were recorded in Europe excluding the UK, and around €300 million in the UK alone (Ziegler et al., 2019). Despite the importance of equity crowdfunding, it has not been a major topic of research until recently. The small body of work that exists focuses on investigating two main aspects of this phenomenon. The main part of it explores the effects of validity signs on investors' behaviour (Agrawal et al., 2016; Lukkarinen et al., 2016; Vismara, 2018); the other strand of work, which is more recent, tends to focus on assessing companies' financial performance following an equity crowdfunding campaign (see, e.g. Signori and Vismara, 2018; Walthoff-Borm et al., 2018; Cumming et al., 2019).

The first stream of work looks at how crowd funders make their investment decisions and evaluate the information related to the company founders and the project when deciding about their investment. Much of this work relies signalling theory (Spence, 1973) to explain why certain projects are favoured over others. Signalling theory states that certain signals of quality, for instance human and social capital cues (Ahlers et al., 2015), are effective for conveying the quality of the venture and the overall likelihood of success in raising capital (Anglin et al., 2018; Plummer et al., 2016).

One of the first studies to investigate quality signals in the context of equity crowdfunding was Ahlers et al. (2015), which examines the impact of project quality on the success of Australian equity crowdfunding campaigns. They found that the entrepreneur's human capital matters for attracting a higher number of investors and that the provision of detailed information on the company, such as financial roadmaps, risk factors, and internal governance, reduce information asymmetries and increase commitment – leading, in turn, to a higher probability of successfully closing a funding round. In the context of the impact of human capital, Piva and Rossi-Lamastra (2018) study the effects of diverse human capital signals on entrepreneurs' success in equity crowdfunding and find that the entrepreneurs' business education and entrepreneurial experience contribute significantly to their success in equity crowdfunding. Confirming this, Nitani et al. (2019) show that crowd investors try to reduce their risk by choosing larger firms, with experienced and educated management with a relatively large equity stake post-offering.

In a study of project characteristics, Mahmood et al. (2019) found that the higher the complexity of the firm's logo was linked to perceived company innovativeness and a higher probability of successfully closing an equity crowdfunding round. Vismara (2019) looked at the influence of sustainable projects on equity crowdfunding. Vismara found that a sustainability orientation does not increase the chances of engaging professional investors and argues that these types of investors follow a market logic whereas crowd investors also consider the community effect. These results are confirmed by Cosma et al. (2019) in their study of social enterprise listings on equity crowdfunding in Italy where they found a lower probability of being financed.

Since in equity crowdfunding investors are less likely to finance firms whose quality is difficult to assess, several studies look at the involvement of professional investor as signalling company quality. Agrawal et al. (2016) investigate the effect of syndicates, that is, groups of investors who lead investment in start-ups, for reducing information asymmetries and acting as a signal of quality for other individual investors and promoting a successful fundraising. Ralcheva and Roosenboom (2016) suggest that companies with business angels backing, which are awarded grants, and which protect their intellectual property have more chances of successful equity crowdfunding. Wang et al. (2019) examine the interplay between the investment decisions of angels and the crowd. They find angels play an important role in the funding of large ventures and that crowd not only fills funding gaps for large ventures but also plays a pivotal role in funding of small firms. They found that angel pledges signal and provide information to the crowd which fosters investment. Cumming et al. (2019) look at the influence of assigning different categories of shares to the crowd and find that a higher separation between ownership and control rights reduces the probability of successful finding.

Several works look at the influence of entrepreneurs' social capital and use of social media on crowdfunding campaign success. Vismara (2016) uses a sample of 271 projects listed on the UK platforms, Crowdcube and Seedrs, in the period 2011–2014 and shows that campaigns launched by entrepreneurs who both retain majority control over their companies at listing and have diverse social networks are more likely to be successful. In a follow-up study, Vismara (2018) shows the importance information cascading down among individual investors in crowdfunding campaigns. The attractiveness of the offer increases if early investors have a public profile, which, in turn, attracts more late investors. Also, Lukkarinen et al. (2016) show that early funding derived from private networks and social media networks, and the size of the minimum investment amount set by the entrepreneur, are associated to campaign success. They found that business-to-consumer (B2C) companies, having a higher degree of understandability, are more likely to be financed by crowd investors. Similarly, Nevin et al. (2017), focusing on the role of social media activities in equity crowdfunding campaign success, show that being active on social media and understanding social media selectivity – that is, using different social media depending on the target audience – have a positive impact on the outcome of the crowdfunding campaign. Nitani et al. (2019) report that firms' and entrepreneurs' social networks have a strong influence on crowd investment decisions.

There is another strand of the literature which looks at the interactions and information exchange between entrepreneurs and potential investors during the fundraising period, and the contribution this makes to reducing information asymmetries. Block et al. (2018) analyse 71 funding campaigns on two German equity crowdfunding portals and find that posting updates on the start-up's latest developments, including new funding, business activity, and cooperation, has a significant positive effect on the number of crowd investments. They find also that clear concise language describing these activities increases crowd participation and that long-winded updates have no effect. Moritz et al. (2015) indicate that perceived sympathy, openness, and trustworthiness of company founders derived from investor communications are important to reduce information asymmetries and incentivise crowd investments. Kleinert and Volkmann (2019) provide a deeper discussion and investigate topics, such as company valuation, financial forecasts, potential returns, shareholder rights, and market risk; they find that these aspects foster investment. However, discussion of market risks and shareholder rights is harmful to funding success.

In studies of the importance of geographical proximity, Agrawal et al. (2015) and Hornuf and Schmitt (2016) suggest that equity crowdfunding investors exhibit local bias, even when controlling for family and friends. In addition to regular crowd investors, their samples include angel-like investors, which invest considerable amounts and exhibit greater local bias. Mohammadi and Shafi (2018) looked at the effect of gender on new venture financing. Using data from a Swedish equity crowdfunding platform, they found that female investors are less likely to invest in young and high-tech firms, confirming the greater risk aversion of female versus male investors.

Table 6.1 summarises the main factors influencing equity crowdfunding campaign success.

TABLE 6.1 Success factors in equity crowdfunding

Founders characteristics	*Company characteristics*	*Investors characteristics*
• Business education • Entrepreneurial experience • Social capital • Social network • Active use of social media • Social media selectivity	• Financial roadmaps • Risk factors • Internal governance • % of equity offered • (Founders retain large equity stake post-offering) • Innovativeness • Understandability of the product	• Syndicates of investors • Presence of angel investors • Investors with a public profile • Engagement with company funders during fundraising

Securing funds is just the first goal of an entrepreneur, aiming to build and grow his/her business. Very few studies examine the post-funding phase and how companies that raised crowdfunding perform. Signori and Vismara (2016) looked at the post-funding performance of crowd-backed companies in the UK and quantified the return on investment in equity crowdfunding. The authors find that 10% of crowd funded firms failed and 30% pursued one or more private equity offers. Signori and Vismara also calculated the expected annual return for an initial crowdfunding investor as 8.8%, implying an overall annual value creation of £25 million.

Walthoff-Borm et al. (2018) investigate the characteristics of firms that choose crowdfunding and find that, overall, these firms consider crowdfunding as a "last resort" since their lack internal funds, poorer capacity for debt and high intangible assets prevent them from accessing other financing possibilities. Hornuf et al. (2018) look at whether equity crowdfunded companies ultimately build enduring businesses. Their findings, from an empirical analysis of various factors related to follow-up funding and firm failure, show that German firms that received equity crowdfunding had a higher chance of obtaining follow-up business angels or venture capitalist funding, but also a higher likelihood of failure. Eldridge et al. (2019) investigate whether equity crowdfunding acts as a catalyst for innovation and growth.Their findings show that crowdfunding has no significant influence on innovation in small firms in the UK, but does have an impact on the growth and overall performance of small firms.

These studies provide a basis that allows an understanding of how crowd investors make decisions and how project characteristics affect the probability of successful fundraising. Despite the limited number, there is some recent research that acknowledges the importance of equity crowdfunding for securing follow-on finance (see Section 7.1 for a comprehensive review of the literature).

6.2 Crowd investors as a source of knowledge and network

Section 6.1 shows the growing interest among academics and practitioners on understanding the impact of equity crowdfunding for helping new ventures to overcome their financial constraints and develop their business. Section 6.2

investigates the role played by crowd investors in supporting development of the company after the initial fundraising round.

Both academics and practitioners consider investors as crucial drivers of entrepreneurial firm success (e.g. Hellmann and Puri, 2002; Sapienza, 1992) through the provision of access to critical resources. The resource-based theory of the firm (Penrose, 1959; Barney, 1986) suggests that firms' competitive advantage depends on their heterogeneous resources both tangible, such as assets, capital, etc., and intangible managers' entrepreneurial capabilities (Grant, 1996; Penrose, 1959). These aspects have been linked to enhanced firm performance, growth, and competitiveness.

New firms suffer from the liability of newness and need to access external resources to survive. The notion of liability of newness was proposed by Stinchcombe (1965) to describe the propensity of younger organizations to show higher rates of failure than their older counterparts. The liability of newness can derive from both internal and external factors (Choi and Shepherd, 2005; Singh et al., 1986; Stinchcombe, 1965). Internal firm factors include the learning costs related to new tasks, the absence of formal organizational routines, lack of trust among new members, and inability to attract skilled labour (Singh et al., 1986; Stinchcombe, 1965). External factors refer to the various forms of barriers to entry such as established organizations' brand recognition and market acceptance, lack of external legitimacy (Singh et al., 1986), and problems related to obtaining loans and equity capital in the external market due to information asymmetries between potential borrowers and lenders (Coleman and Cohn, 2000). Thus, the ability of new ventures to leverage external networks for resources acquisition and exploitation could ensure their survival (Autio et al., 2000; West and Noel, 2009).

In recent years, several empirical works have added to our understanding of the importance of external knowledge sources for new ventures. Among the various providers of resources, the entrepreneurial finance literature highlights professional investors, such as venture capitalists, corporate venture capitalist, business angels, etc., for supporting the growth, productivity, and innovation activities of new ventures (Wright and Robbie, 1998; Colombo and Grilli, 2010).

Investors are seen as important for facilitating new ventures' access to non-financial resources, such as business and industry knowledge, managerial skills, and networks (e.g. Hellmann and Puri, 2002; Dutta and Folta, 2016; Politis, 2008), which are fundamental for overcoming the liability of newness (Stinchcombe, 1965).

Venture capitalists provide portfolio companies with consultancy services in various fields including strategic planning, marketing, finance, accounting, and human resources management (Baum and Silverman, 2004; MacMillan et al., 1989; Sapienza, 1992; Barney et al., 1996; Sapienza et al., 1996; Lerner, 1995). New ventures are able to exploit venture capitalists' networks, which include potential customers, suppliers, and alliance partners (Bertoni et al., 2011). Therefore, portfolio firms may find it easier to access external resources and competencies out of the reach of other new ventures (Colombo et al., 2006;

Hsu, 2006; Bottazzi et al., 2008). These value-adding services are especially important for early stage firms in high-tech industries (Aspelund et al., 2005).

Bertoni et al. (2011) analyse the impact of venture capitalists on the growth of Italian new ventures. Their results provide clear support for the view that venture capitalists have a large positive effect on the growth of firm's employment and sales. Numerous empirical studies demonstrate the importance of the investors' involvement in day-to-day managerial decisions and the impact on new ventures' financial performance (Croce et al., 2013; Jackson et al., 2012; Bottazzi et al., 2008).

These non-financial resources are seminal for new ventures for two reasons. First, knowledge resources are fundamental to competitive advantage. At the outset, the entrepreneur may lack knowledge about the environment, employees' commitment, and relationships with customers and suppliers, which makes the new organization vulnerable (Stinchcombe, 1965; Yli-Renko et al., 2001). Second, knowledge resources lead to the development of other important resources such as financial and physical capital (Brush et al., 2001). Therefore, the ability of new ventures to leverage external networks, such as the crowd investor network, to obtain additional intangible resources, could foster survival and growth (Autio et al., 2000; West and Noel, 2009).

As discussed in Chapter 5, despite the benefits professional investors provide to new ventures, it can be difficult for the new venture in the early development phase to attract professional investors and obtain the benefits derived from their "value-added" services. In this context, equity crowdfunding helps the new company to overcome its financial gap and raise enough funding to develop the business, test the market, and create a customer base (see Sections 5.2 and 5.3, for a detailed analysis of the benefits of listing on equity crowdfunding). However, apart from providing the initial funding, the crowd network has the potential to act as a think-tank and to support further business development. For instance, the crowd may take an active role in the firm's management and provide the entrepreneur with the knowledge and capabilities critical for success.

Due to the importance of equity crowdfunding in early-stage financing of new ventures, we investigate the additional benefits that crowd investors can provide to the venture after initial fundraising.

Some entrepreneurs recognize the importance of the crowd as an important source of information. For instance, several companies that sought financial capital on the US equity-crowdfunding platform, CircleUp, have benefited from their funders in other ways. In particular, the start-up 18Rabbits received valuable feedback on packaging and site design from some experienced investors, which enhanced its sales; Willa Sinkcare received help from investors when hiring a CFO; and NativeFlow was introduced to a potential strategic partner in Japan (Forbes, 2014). These examples suggest that crowd investors' knowledge and networks can be leveraged by entrepreneurs to facilitate access to tangible and intangible resources needed to grow the business.

To obtain more information on the potential value of the crowd, we conducted a study of companies listed on equity-based European crowdfunding platforms to investigate the involvement of crowd investors in the companies after the close of the fundraising round. We employed a qualitative methodology, often used to explore areas where little is known (Strauss and Corbin, 1998; Stern, 1980); our primary source of data was interviews. We conducted 60 in '-depth semi-structured interviews – both face-to-face and via Skype, with entrepreneurs listed on equity crowdfunding platforms in the UK, the Netherlands, France, Finland, and Sweden. The interviews were based on a semi-structured interview protocol, and we encouraged respondents to provide detailed answers and examples in response to our questions. We asked our interviewees to describe the company activities in which their investors were involved; which competences or information they provided; and the influence of investor involvement on the firm's development. We collected archival data (newspaper articles, business interviews, and crowdfunding-platform data) on each firm to obtain the firms' crowdfunding experience.

The companies in our sample were from a range of different industries, including food and beverage, high-tech, finance, fitness, fashion, real estate, among others, and were in different development phases – some had reached pre-commercialisation, others had already started selling their products, while some others were looking to expand the business.

We used a grounded theory approach to analyse our data (Strauss and Corbin, 1998). We constructed categories representing the contributions of crowd investors to different firm activities. Table 6.2 reports our main categories derived from the data analysis process.

Depending on the type and outcome of contribution, we categorised crowd involvement as light or deep involvement. Deep involvement included a hands-on approach such as involvement of the crowd in activities aimed at developing the product and the firm strategically. Light involvement includes crowd support through provision of general business advice, providing links to external stakeholders, and acting as business ambassador to raise awareness of the firm.

Figure 6.1 is a conceptual model based on analysis of our empirical observations.

The results of our study demonstrate that crowd investors provide entrepreneurs with complementary knowledge and information useful to develop the

TABLE 6.2 Contributions of crowd equity investors in company activities

- Providing product feedback
- Participating in defining the growth strategy of the company
- Establishing partnership
- Obtaining additional financing
- Providing connections with potential clients and investors
- Promoting the product/business to external stakeholders

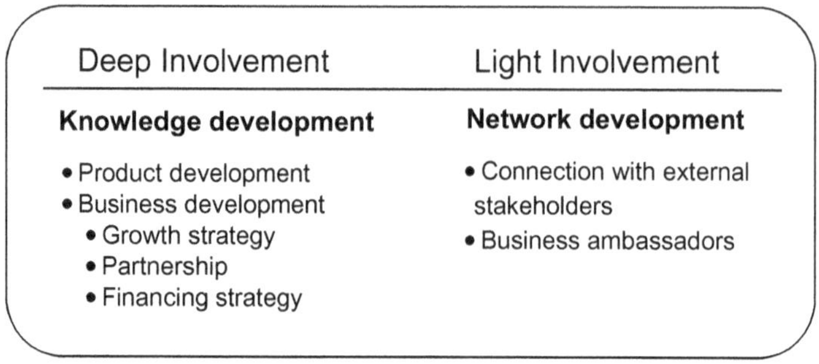

FIGURE 6.1 Crowd equity investors: deep and light involvement in company activities

new venture. New firms can exploit the crowd's knowledge by involving crowd funders in developments at an early stage. The next two sub-sections provide some examples and discussion the involvement categories identified.

6.2.1 Deep involvement: product and business development

The deep-involvement category includes involvement in company activities related to product development and business development. By product development we mean activities related to improving and finalising the product, before commercialisation; business development refers to activities related to defining the firm's strategic development. Around 70% of the entrepreneurs interviewed reported involvement their investors in activities related to either product or business development or both.

6.2.1.1 Product development

Investors contribute to product finalisation based on the prototype, through the provision of feedback and sharing of experience as users on beta-versions. This increases the new firm's knowledge about customer needs. Some entrepreneurs gave examples of investor involvement in technology-related aspects and experience. One entrepreneur, based in London, explained that:

> You get this community of people interest in your project and you are able to exploit this collective intelligence. You can ask questions and say: what do you think about this? And they give you feedback. And I think this is very important. We were able to put things out to the crowd and get some general feedback, we have expertise, but it is important to constantly develop the product. We got some investors who had some really useful inputs in terms of things to consider and some useful feedback on the product itself: how we deal with the product, how we develop the product, how we build it around user's experience. This has been really useful. Company A, Founder.

The founder of a company app, which offers a list of fitness classes and activities available on demand in London, involved investors in testing the functionality of the technology implemented before making it available online to customers. The founder reported:

> We will launch the product in a couple of weeks and some of our investors are involved as testers. So, we have been live by testing the app now and few people who invested are booking and attending classes, and give us feedback on the booking and experience process. Company B, Founder.

Some entrepreneurs consulted the crowd for advice and suggestions on marketing and websites. The managing director of a real estate company, who believes in exploiting the crowd's collective intelligence and considers it valuable for firm growth and success said:

> We are involving our investors to early test our approaches to marketing and websites. We also were looking for ideas to identify a model maker and we had couple of responses from crowd funders. It is an on-going process and we do use them as a resource. Company C, MD.

6.2.1.2 Business development

In addition to crowdfunding investors' in product development activities, our study suggests strategic-level involvement in these businesses. Specifically, some investors have been involved in defining the firm's business development strategy, offering their heterogeneous expertise to the entrepreneur and suggestions related to its growth strategy. Some investors were members of the firms' executive boards while others were more interested in strategic-partnerships. One respondent told us:

> Some investors are involved in our growth strategy. Their knowledge is much more around business development; we had some thoughts in term of business strategy and our growth strategy. We got some really useful perspective; they have very interesting level of experience. Company A, Founder

The founder of a company specialised in gourmet-quality pizzas had received input from the crowd about how to redefine its expansion strategy and expressions of interest in establishing partnerships to expand the business internationally. The firm founder explained:

> One of our bigger investors, who is also in the company board, has restaurants in South America and he is interested in taking the franchising of our company in Brazil. Another investor, who is an entrepreneur and founder of a consultancy company, offered me support for defining the business development strategy of the company and in the future; she is interested in taking the franchising to open shops outside London. Company D, Founder

The founder of a tortilla factory in Dublin, producing high-quality corn tortillas for the European market, talked about the benefits of having passionate investors who see things from a different perspective and increase the rate of growth of the business. He reported that:

> One of our investors actually became the operation director of the company. He is really accomplishing individual, he is very enthusiastic, has a lot of knowledge, and is eager to work. It is great to have him involved. Another investor would be assisting with the expansion into the European market. He has a very large contacts-base on the distributors and supply chain. Thanks to this particular individual we can really leverage the growth rate a lot. Company E, Founder.

In some cases, crowdfunding investors had supported the new venture by finding additional sources of finance after the initial crowdfunding campaign or had established partnerships and were offering complementary services. For instance, the founder of a sports and fitness classes business, based in London, explained:

> One of our investors invested again, he gave us more money and a couple of them helped me to obtain additional financing. One investor is in the medical space, so I reach out to him to fit into his program. Company F, Founder.

The empirical evidence demonstrates how young organizations and first-time entrepreneurs can leverage investors' expertise to finalise development of their product and the firm's strategic choices. Crowdfunding investors can be involved actively in providing knowledge and feedback on product development and growth strategy. Our study shows that the crowd offers feedback during product development, provides suggestions about potential technological improvements, and offers marketing-related and general advice. This level of involvement renders investors co-creators of the product. Entrepreneurs fine-tune their product development taking account of and building on the crowd's feedback, suggestions, and experience. In terms of strategic involvement, investors' expertise is useful to identify the firm's potential development and growth strategy including international expansion through partnership with investors with industry experience.

Investors provide intangible value to the new venture. This intangible value is critical in the early stages, since early-stage companies rely on the knowledge resources of founders (Brush et al., 2001). Knowledge resources include understanding how to start a new organization, how to manage people and processes, how to achieve growth and competitive position, and how to stage technology and new product development (Brush et al., 2001; Wiklund and Shepherd, 2005). The entrepreneur's idiosyncratic experience can lead to a narrow view of available opportunities, which may not be optimal for company growth. To reduce uncertainty, entrepreneurs are encouraged to supplement the industry, business, or previous start-up knowledge with additional knowledge from external sources (West and Noel, 2009). In this regards, crowdfunding investors are a rich source of knowledge which the young organization can tap into. Hence, our analysis implies that equity crowdfunding has the potential to facilitate and accelerate the accumulation of additional knowledge lacked by the entrepreneur to enable sustainable competitive advantage (Stinchcombe, 1965). Knowledge accumulation requires time and investment, and in order to keep pace with environmental changes, entrepreneurs need to move fast and to compensate for missing skills by tapping into external sources to avoid problems related to capacity to cope with difficulties and identify new opportunities. In this case, equity crowd investors can be a valuable external source of market and business-related knowledge and information for the entrepreneur.

6.2.2 Light involvement: connection with external stakeholders and business ambassadors

The light-involvement category includes crowd involvement in company activities related to the exploitation of equity investor networks in order to increase awareness of the business and establish relationships with external stakeholders, such as industry partners and investors.

Connection with stakeholders: our respondents reported that crowd investors had been critical for establishing external connections with industry players and future investors. One explained that:

> I keep reaching out to crowd investors asking them to help me to connect with relevant people for my business. What we are trying to do right now is to lunch a corporate wellness function that means health & benefits to corporates. Company F, founder.

The crowd is also useful for providing contacts with suppliers of materials and potential retailers, as the founder of a Finnish ice-cream company explained:

> Crowd investors sent us information about a more affordable packaging material, he is from Estonia and it seems that he could make a really good price for us. Then these investors helped us to get more retailers. Company G, co-founder.

In addition to facilitating connections with external partners, crowd investors are critical for providing the firm with visibility. A successful crowdfunding campaign allowed entrepreneurs to develop a customer base for their product and promote it pre-commercialisation. The founder reported:

> The people who are investing are not just normal customers, they are community members, they are very enthusiastic and passionate about what we do, they don't just buy the product, they go through extraordinary lenses to get you in the stores in their local neighbours, to give you introductions to people that might help you to export or distribute the product. Company E, founder.

6.2.2.1 Business ambassadors

Crowdfunding investors were considered by our respondents as useful for promoting the business and the product. After completion of the product development phase, the crowd was useful to advertise the product. Many respondents reported that investors acted as business ambassadors, spreading news about the company on their social media, and via friends, family, etc. One respondent reported that:

> The best thing is that they are evangelist of the product; once the start-up is running, there is nothing better that word of mouth that multiply by 20 the potential customers. Company H, founder.

The founder of an international career consultant company admitted that he had not had the opportunity to engage the crowd in the company's activities, but could see its potential and intended to exploit it in the near future. He reported:

> I think it is definitely useful to have them, we haven't use them yet, but I think is because we haven't had the right opportunity to exploit their potential. I think when we will launch the campaign around the new courses that we are implementing we will definitely use them to help promoting and lunch new things. Company I founder.

The founder of a dating app explained the importance of the crowd for promoting the company brand and described the importance of the emotional attachment of investors to the company. He reported that:

> We love having close relationship and frequent communications with our investors especially now that we have a build a brand; this is the best way to promote your name. These people are very influential, they have thousand people next to them, in their circles, and so without them I think the risk to fail is ten times larger. The crowd behaves completely different from professional investors, they are getting hooked not because of the opportunity because of the attractiveness that this concept has. Company L, founder.

We found that equity crowd investors are important for facilitating company connections to external stakeholders. One of the first tasks of any nascent venture is to gain legitimacy in its sector, acceptance, and validation from external stakeholders (Singh et al., 1986; Stinchcombe, 1965). Our study shows that crowdfunding investors play a significant role in enhancing the external legitimacy of new ventures. Specifically, crowd funders are interested in establishing partnerships with entrepreneurs, leveraging their networks to connect the entrepreneur with relevant others, providing help to find materials suppliers, product retailers, and easing access to other sources of financing.

The crowd may invest more of its resources or facilitate links to other potential investors. Liquidity can buffer against the liabilities of newness, and reassure and encourage potential external stakeholders to invest.

Another important aspect is business promotion. Crowd funders can increase the new venture's popularity and brand recognition. In line with Lambert and Schwienbacher's (2010) argument that crowdfunding is an inexpensive way to raise awareness, investors reported that funders act as ambassadors for the business; they spread the word; they promote the product and the business via social media and friends, and increase the company's visibility.

6.2.3 *Final reflection: tapping into the crowd's knowledge and network*

The results of this study provide insights into how new ventures benefit from external sources of knowledge, especially equity crowd investors, and contributes to our understanding of the equity crowdfunding phenomenon. Crowdfunding and its underlying concept, Web 2.0, allows participation, collaboration, and communication between investors and new ventures and, thus, knowledge exchange. Crowd participation affects new venture development and growth and contributes, in particular, to knowledge and network development (see Figure 6.1).

The investigation in this chapter implies that equity crowdfunding has the potential to facilitate accumulation of knowledge that the entrepreneur lacks, and to supplement the entrepreneur's existing knowledge to create sustainable competitive advantage (West and Noel, 2009). We show, also, the importance of crowdfunding investors for developing the new venture's network, increasing company visibility, and creating connections with potential customers, clients, and investors. Thus, the crowd can help new organizations to achieve external acceptance and validation.

We have shown that crowdfunding is more than an alternative way to raise funds (Lambert and Schwienbacher, 2010): new ventures can make use of the crowd and can benefit from its collective intelligence. Crowdfunding is also an external source of knowledge for both experienced and first-time entrepreneurs. Given the importance of knowledge for new firm survival, and since the crowd can facilitate access to external knowledge, entrepreneurs should consider those aspects when making decisions about crowdfunding.

6.3 Challenges related to crowd investors exploitation: the role of proximity

Section 6.2 highlighted the benefits, in terms of knowledge accumulation and network exploitation, obtained by entrepreneurs from the crowd funder community. The literature agrees that collaboration with stakeholders is beneficial and necessary for the start-up, and compensates for lack of internal resources and competences (Aldrich and Auster, 1986; Stinchcombe, 1965; Alvarez and Busenitz, 2001; Lichtenstein and Brush, 2001). However, exploiting external resources, such as crowd investors, can be difficult for new ventures for several reasons (Salter et al., 2014), related to both their firm-level capabilities (Alexy et al., 2012) and their employees and managers' attitudes (Schierjott et al., 2018).

A recent strand of work highlights the role of organizational design for integrating external knowledge in the firm, facilitating interactions with external knowledge sources, and exploiting opportunities (Jansen et al., 2005). For instance, Foss et al. (2011) suggest that use of new organisational practices – namely, vertical and lateral communication, rewarding employees for sharing and acquiring knowledge, and delegation of decision rights – makes it easier for firms to access customer knowledge. Also, establishing direct channels of communication with external sources via dedicated departments, or interdependencies with internal technology investments, facilitates use of external knowledge (Heimeriks et al., 2007; Noseleit and de Faria, 2013; Wassmer, 2010; Wuyts and Dutta, 2014; Antonelli and Colombelli, 2015). In addition to firm-level capabilities, the firm's engagement with external sources is influenced by employees' and managers' attitudes (Schierjott et al., 2018; Katz and Allen, 1982; Agrawal et al., 2010; Chesbrough, 2003). Also, external relationships can depend on the entrepreneur's personal links and willingness to engage with external parties (Ahn et al., 2017).

Despite the constraints on external knowledge exploitation highlighted in the literature, the crowdfunding context is characterised by peculiarities that lead to the emergence of other potential challenges related to exploiting crowd investors to obtain external knowledge. We discuss the issues linked to: (i) crowd investors' characteristics; and (ii) Internet-based transactions.

We propose a theoretical framework to explain equity investors' exploitation and linkages, using a proximity lens. Proximity, Boschma (2005) suggests, is a multidimensional concept, which includes geographical proximity (same spatial area), cognitive proximity (same knowledge base), and social proximity (common relationships). It is suggested, also, that proximity, in some (but not necessarily all) of its dimensions, is required to promote connections among actors and to enable learning and knowledge exchange.

In what follows, we explain our conceptual model and the different forms of proximity that can hamper or facilitate knowledge transfer between entrepreneurs and the crowd.

6.3.1 Geographical, social, and cognitive proximity

Geographical proximity between the new venture and its partners is considered an important parameter that the new venture can use to exploit external knowledge (Alcácer and Chung, 2007; Audretsch and Lehmann, 2006). Geographical proximity influences information exchange by increasing the probability of collaboration, by producing spontaneous, social, and professional interactions, and by increasing the probability of face-to-face interactions (Dyer and Nobeoka, 2000). In the context of electronic commerce, the literature shows that, although the cost of the distance between buyers and sellers is reduced, information-related costs exist and remain an important impediment to remote transactions (Blum and Goldfarb, 2006; Gomez-Herrera et al., 2014; Hortaçsu et al., 2009). The importance of geographical proximity is also addressed in work on crowdfunding. Prior work shows that distance matters for crowdfunding investment decisions, and that online transactions are more likely between buyers and sellers in the same geographical area (see, e.g. Agrawal et al., 2011, 2015; Ordanini et al., 2011; Lin and Viswanathan, 2015; Hortaçsu et al., 2009). Non-local investors are disadvantaged, relative to local investors, in their access to local information, networks, capital, and resources and, typically, incur higher information asymmetries and transaction costs (Guenther et al., 2018; Jaffe et al., 1993; Thompson and Fox-Kean, 2005; Ordanini et al., 2011; Hornuf and Schmitt, 2016; Boschma, 2005; Agrawal et al., 2011).

In line with the argument in the extant literature that geographical proximity helps to reduce information asymmetry and facilitates interactions and collaboration, we posit that equity crowd funders located in the same geographical area as the entrepreneur will be more likely to be involved in company activities.

> *Proposition 1: Geographical proximity between crowd investors and entrepreneurs will encourage exploitation of crowd investors knowledge.*

However, recent studies suggest that geographical proximity cannot be assessed in isolation. Geographical proximity per se is neither a necessary nor a sufficient condition for the process of knowledge acquisition (Boschma, 2005; Antonelli, 2000), since other nontangible dimensions of proximity can act as substitutes for geographical proximity (Boschma, 2005; Rallet and Torre, 1999; Boschma and Lambooy, 1999). In particular, these authors argue that the importance of geographical proximity will be weakened if the partners share the same cognitive experience (cognitive proximity) and if the relationship between partners is socially embedded and, thus, is characterised by a high level of trust (social proximity) – and especially in the case of tacit knowledge. This justifies our interest in the other two dimensions of proximity.

The notion of cognitive proximity suggests people sharing the same knowledge base and expertise can learn from each other (Boschma, 2005). The effective transfer of knowledge requires absorptive capacity to identify, interpret, and exploit new knowledge (Cohen and Levinthal, 1990). Thus, actors' or firms' capacity to absorb new knowledge requires cognitive proximity because this facilitates effective communication (Boschma, 2005).

Similarity knowledge stocks enhances the transfer of knowledge while differences tend to delay or prevent the absorption of the partner's knowledge (Lane and Lubatkin, 1998). Empirical studies confirm the positive effect of cognitive proximity on knowledge exploitation (Huber, 2012; Molina-Morales et al., 2014; Dakhli and de Clercq, 2004; Presutti et al., 2011).

This is true, specifically, in the context of crowdfunding, which presents certain other peculiarities. Among these is the fact that entrepreneurs cannot choose their crowd investors. Therefore, lack of knowledge specific to the business is another reason for low or lack of involvement with investor communities. Specifically, start-ups at an embryonic stage of development need mentoring and support related to how to run the business, and expertise in the focal business sector. Entrepreneurs look to establish relationships with people with such expertise and an understanding of the critical components of the business proposition.

If the similarities in actors' knowledge is low – that is, the cognitive proximity between crowd investors and entrepreneurs is small – this can generate low levels of external engagement activities.

Therefore, we posit:

> *Proposition 2: Cognitive proximity between crowd investors and entrepreneurs will encourage exploitation of crowd investors' knowledge.*

Lastly, the concept of social proximity derives from the literature on embeddedness (Granovetter, 1985), which states that relationships between partners are socially embedded if they involve a high level of trust. The presence of trust in the business relationship allows more efficient reciprocal knowledge acquisition because it reduces the risks of opportunistic behaviour and encouraged informal relations which are considered more effective for acquiring external knowledge (Nahapiet and Ghoshal, 1998). A tie based on high levels of reciprocal trust reinforces the process of knowledge exploitation (Presutti et al., 2011; Agrawal et al., 2008).

In the crowdfunding context, the importance of social proximity has been investigated in relation to predicting successful crowdfunding fundraising (Agrawal et al., 2015). Friends and family ties represent an important share of the financial support from crowdfunding (Mollick, 2014). This strand of work acknowledges the relevance of social ties and trust among proponents and fundraisers, over the geographical proximity among the parties. This result is important since it shows that social ties are more significant than distance for explaining the decision to invest in a project.

In the case of involvement of crowd investors in the post-funding phase, lack of trust is often a major deterrent to effective external engagement in crowdfunding. Faced with the impossibility of choosing among and controlling who is included in the crowd, the entrepreneurs may find it difficult to identify genuine interest in investing in the company versus potential competitors seeking access to sensitive company information. Revealing company information related to products, growth strategy, partnerships, fundraising, etc., to large numbers of unknown people can be problematic. Because crowdfunding reaches a very broad audience through the web, it lacks the trust involved in traditional fundraising through private transactions with professional investors. Therefore, entrepreneurs are likely to be more willing to engage with crowd investors if they establish a personal relationship with them and can organise face to face meetings to allow the entrepreneur to assess the investors' interest in the company. Therefore, we posit:

> *Proposition 3: Social proximity between crowd investors and entrepreneurs will encourage exploitation of crowd investors' knowledge.*

Figure 6.2 depicts the conceptual model of different forms of proximity and their influence on exploiting crowd investors as external knowledge sources.

In a globalising world where new technologies promote and facilitate mobility of resources (Aizenman and Kendall, 2012; Agrawal et al., 2015; Lin and Viswanathan, 2016), we would argue that distance-related economic frictions remain a strong barrier to resources and knowledge exchanges (Nahata et al., 2014; Li et al., 2014; Dai et al., 2012; Lin and Viswanathan, 2016; Siegel et al., 2011; Hornuf and Schmitt, 2016; Liu and Maula, 2016), for both economic (e.g. information asymmetries and transactions costs) and behavioural reasons (including familiarity bias and trust in local opportunities) (Huberman, 2001; Lai and Teo, 2008; Strong and Xu, 2003). However, other form of proximity, such as social and cognitive proximity, may moderate the negative impact of geographical distance and favour exchanges of resources and knowledge.

Social relationships tend to exist not just in physical space but also in social space (Sorenson, 2018). Thus, people tend to have relationships with similar others – similar religion, culture, education level, and with experience in the same types of firms and industries (Miller McPherson et al., 2001). Therefore, leveraging social ties facilitates the creation of networks, enhances trust, and increase the chances of cooperation (Lim and Putnam, 2010) between crowd investors and the entrepreneur.

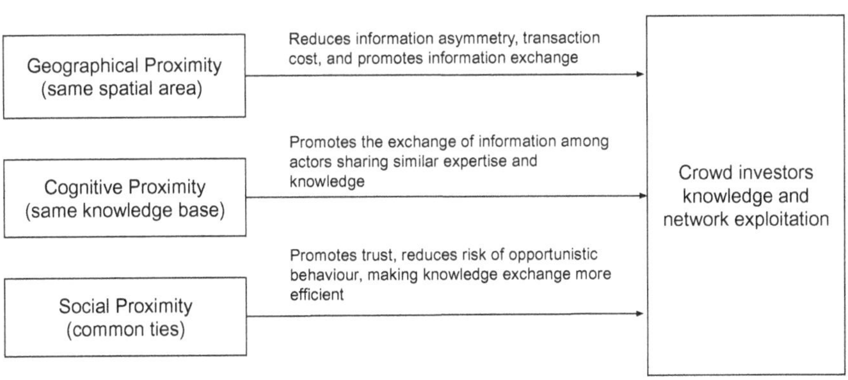

FIGURE 6.2 The influence of different forms of proximity on crowd investors' knowledge exploitation

Also, very important for establishing relationships with external stakeholders, such as crowd investors, is a common knowledge base. Crowd investors offer a range of expertise and knowledge which the entrepreneur can tap into. It is important, therefore, for the entrepreneur to investigate investors' profiles to identify what they can bring to the company and how their expertise can be leveraged to support firm development.

References

Agrawal, A., Catalini, C. and Goldfarb, A., 2015. Crowdfunding: Geography, social networks, and the timing of investment decisions. *Journal of Economics & Management Strategy, 24*(2), pp. 253–274.

Agrawal, A., Catalini, C. and Goldfarb, A., 2016. Are syndicates the killer app of equity crowdfunding? *California Management Review, 58*(2), pp. 111–124.

Agrawal, A., Cockburn, I. and Rosell, C., 2010. Not invented here? Innovation in company towns. *Journal of Urban Economics, 67*(1), pp. 78–89.

Agrawal, A., Kapur, D. and McHale, J., 2008. How do spatial and social proximity influence knowledge flows? Evidence from patent data. *Journal of Urban Economics, 64*(2), pp. 258–269.

Agrawal, A.K., Catalini, C. and Goldfarb, A., 2011. *The Geography of Crowdfunding* (No. w16820). National Bureau of Economic Research, Cambridge, MA.

Ahlers, G.K., Cumming, D., Günther, C. and Schweizer, D., 2015. Signaling in equity crowdfunding. *Entrepreneurship Theory and Practice, 39*(4), pp. 955–980.

Ahn, J.M., Minshall, T. and Mortara, L., 2017. Understanding the human side of openness: The fit between open innovation modes and CEO characteristics. *R&D Management, 47*(5), pp. 727–740.

Aizenman, J. and Kendall, J., 2012. The internationalization of venture capital. *Journal of Economic Studies, 39*(5), pp. 488–511.

Alcácer, J. and Chung, W., 2007. Location strategies and knowledge spillovers. *Management Science, 53*(5), pp. 760–776.

Aldrich, H. and Auster, E.R., 1986. Even dwarfs started small: Liabilities of age and size and their strategic implications. *Research in Organizational Behavior, 8*, pp. 165–186.

Alexy, O., Criscuolo, P. and Salter, A., 2012. Managing unsolicited ideas for R&D. *California Management Review, 54*(3), pp. 116–139.

Alvarez, S.A. and Busenitz, L.W., 2001. The entrepreneurship of resource-based theory. *Journal of Management, 27*(6), pp. 755–775.

Anglin, A.H., Short, J.C., Drover, W., Stevenson, R.M., McKenny, A.F. and Allison, T.H., 2018. The power of positivity? The influence of positive psychological capital language on crowdfunding performance. *Journal of Business Venturing, 33*(4), pp. 470–492.

Antonelli, C., 2000. Collective knowledge communication and innovation: The evidence of technological districts. *Regional Studies, 34*(6), 535–547.

Antonelli, C. and Colombelli, A., 2015. External and internal knowledge in the knowledge generation function. *Industry and Innovation, 22*(4), pp. 273–298.

Aspelund, A., Berg-Utby, T. and Skjevdal, R., 2005. Initial resources' influence on new venture survival: A longitudinal study of new technology-based firms. *Technovation, 25*(11), pp. 1337–1347.

Audretsch, D.B. and Lehmann, E., 2006. Entrepreneurial access and absorption of knowledge spillovers: Strategic board and managerial composition for competitive advantage. *Journal of Small Business Management, 44*(2), pp. 155–166.

Autio, E., Sapienza, H.J. and Almeida, J.G., 2000. Effects of age at entry, knowledge intensity, and imitability on international growth. *Academy of Management Journal, 43*(5), pp. 909–924.

Barney, J.B., 1986. Strategic factor markets: Expectations, luck, and business strategy. *Management Science, 32*(10), pp. 1231–1241.

Barney, J.B., Busenitz, L.W., Fiet, J.O. and Moesel, D.D., 1996. New venture teams' assessment of learning assistance from venture capital firms. *Journal of Business Venturing, 11*(4), pp. 257–272.

Baum, J.A. and Silverman, B.S., 2004. Picking winners or building them? Alliance, intellectual, and human capital as selection criteria in venture financing and performance of biotechnology startups. *Journal of Business Venturing, 19*(3), pp. 411–436.

Bertoni, F., Colombo, M.G. and Grilli, L., 2011. Venture capital financing and the growth of high-tech start-ups: Disentangling treatment from selection effects. *Research Policy, 40*(7), pp. 1028–1043.

Block, J., Hornuf, L. and Moritz, A., 2018. Which updates during an equity crowdfunding campaign increase crowd participation? *Small Business Economics, 50*(1), pp. 3–27.

Blum, B.S. and Goldfarb, A., 2006. Does the internet defy the law of gravity? *Journal of International Economics, 70*(2), pp. 384–405.

Boschma, R., 2005. Proximity and innovation: A critical assessment. *Regional Studies, 39*(1), pp. 61–74.

Boschma, R.A. and Lambooy, J.G., 1999. Evolutionary economics and economic geography. *Journal of Evolutionary Economics, 9*(4), pp. 411–429.

Bottazzi, L., Da Rin, M. and Hellmann, T., 2008. Who are the active investors? *Journal of Financial Economics, 3*(89), pp. 488–512.

Brush, C.G., Greene, P.G. and Hart, M.M., 2001. From initial idea to unique advantage: The entrepreneurial challenge of constructing a resource base. *Academy of Management Perspectives, 15*(1), pp. 64–78.

Chesbrough, H., 2003. The logic of open innovation: Managing intellectual property. *California Management Review, 45*(3), pp. 33–58.

Choi, Y.R. and Shepherd, D.A., 2005. Stakeholder perceptions of age and other dimensions of newness. *Journal of Management, 31*(4), pp. 573–596.

Cohen, W.M. and Levinthal, D.A., 1990. Absorptive capacity: A new perspective on learning and innovation. *Administrative Science Quarterly, 35*(1), pp. 128–152.

Coleman, S. and Cohn, R., 2000. Small firms' use of financial leverage: Evidence from the 1993 National Survey of Small Business Finances. *Journal of Business and Entrepreneurship, 12*(3), p. 81.

Colombo, M.G. and Grilli, L., 2010. On growth drivers of high-tech start-ups: Exploring the role of founders' human capital and venture capital. *Journal of Business Venturing, 25*(6), pp. 610–626.

Colombo, M.G., Grilli, L. and Piva, E., 2006. In search of complementary assets: The determinants of alliance formation of high-tech start-ups. *Research Policy, 35*(8), pp. 1166–1199.

Cosma, S., Grasso, A.G., Pagliacci, F. and Pedrazzoli, A., 2019. Is equity crowdfunding a good tool for social enterprises? In *Socially Responsible Investments* (pp. 149–170). Palgrave Pivot, Cham.

Croce, A., Martí, J. and Murtinu, S., 2013. The impact of venture capital on the productivity growth of European entrepreneurial firms: "Screening" or "value added" effect? *Journal of Business Venturing, 28*(4), pp. 489–510.

Cumming, D., Meoli, M. and Vismara, S., 2019. Investors' choices between cash and voting rights: Evidence from dual-class equity crowdfunding. *Research Policy, 48*(8), pp. 2–19.

Dai, N., Jo, H. and Kassicieh, S., 2012. Cross-border venture capital investments in Asia: Selection and exit performance. *Journal of Business Venturing, 27*(6), pp. 666–684.

Dakhli, M. and De Clercq, D., 2004. Human capital, social capital, and innovation: A multi-country study. *Entrepreneurship & Regional Development, 16*(2), pp. 107–128.

Dutta, S. and Folta, T.B., 2016. A comparison of the effect of angels and venture capitalists on innovation and value creation. *Journal of Business Venturing, 31*(1), pp. 39–54.

Dyer, J.H. and Nobeoka, K., 2000. Creating and managing a high-performance knowledge-sharing network: The Toyota case. *Strategic Management Journal, 21*(3), pp. 345–367.

Eldridge, D., Nisar, T.M. and Torchia, M., 2019. What impact does equity crowdfunding have on SME innovation and growth? An empirical study. *Small Business Economics*, pp. 1–16.

Forbes, 2014. Crowdbuilding: The real story behind crowdfunding that no one's telling, January 2013. Zack Miller is the Contributor, https://www.forbes.com/sites/zackmiller/2014/01/13/crowdbuilding-the-real-story-behind-crowdfunding-that-no-ones-telling/.

Foss, N.J., Laursen, K. and Pedersen, T., 2011. Linking customer interaction and innovation: The mediating role of new organizational practices. *Organization Science, 22*(4), pp. 980–999.

Gomez-Herrera, E., Martens, B. and Turlea, G., 2014. The drivers and impediments for cross-border e-commerce in the EU. *Information Economics and Policy, 28*, pp. 83–96.

Granovetter, M., 1985. Economic action and social structure: The problem of embeddedness. *American Journal of Sociology, 91*(3), pp. 481–510.

Grant, R.M., 1996. Toward a knowledge-based theory of the firm. *Strategic Management Journal, 17*(S2), pp. 109–122.

Guenther, C., Johan, S. and Schweizer, D., 2018. Is the crowd sensitive to distance? – How investment decisions differ by investor type. *Small Business Economics, 50*(2), pp. 289–305.

Heimeriks, K.H., Duysters, G. and Vanhaverbeke, W., 2007. Learning mechanisms and differential performance in alliance portfolios. *Strategic Organization, 5*(4), pp. 373–408.

Hellmann, T. and Puri, M., 2002. Venture capital and the professionalization of start-up firms: Empirical evidence. *The Journal of Finance, 57*(1), pp. 169–197.

Hornuf, L. and Schmitt, M., 2016. Does a local bias exist in equity crowdfunding? *Max Planck Institute for Innovation & Competition Research Paper*, 16-07.

Hornuf, L., Schmitt, M. and Stenzhorn, E., 2018. Equity crowdfunding in Germany and the United Kingdom: Follow-up funding and firm failure. *Corporate Governance: An International Review, 26*(5), pp. 331–354.

Hortaçsu, A., Martínez-Jerez, F. and Douglas, J., 2009. The geography of trade in online transactions: Evidence from eBay and MercadoLibre. *American Economic Journal: Microeconomics, 1*(1), pp. 53–74.

Hsu, D.H., 2006. Venture capitalists and cooperative start-up commercialization strategy. *Management Science, 52*(2), pp. 204–219.

Huber, F., 2012. On the role and interrelationship of spatial, social and cognitive proximity: Personal knowledge relationships of R&D workers in the Cambridge information technology cluster. *Regional Studies, 46*(9), pp. 1169–1182.

Huberman, G., 2001. Familiarity breeds investment. *The Review of Financial Studies, 14*(3), pp. 659–680.

Jackson III, W.E., Bates, T. and Bradford, W.D., 2012. Does venture capitalist activism improve investment performance? *Journal of Business Venturing, 27*(3), pp. 342–354.

Jaffe, A.B., Trajtenberg, M. and Henderson, R., 1993. Geographic localization of knowledge spillovers as evidenced by patent citations. *The Quarterly Journal of Economics, 108*(3), pp. 577–598.

Jansen, J.J., Van Den Bosch, F.A. and Volberda, H.W., 2005. Managing potential and realized absorptive capacity: How do organizational antecedents matter? *Academy of Management Journal, 48*(6), pp. 999–1015.

Katz, R. and Allen, T.J., 1982. Investigating the Not Invented Here (NIH) syndrome: A look at the performance, tenure, and communication patterns of 50 R & D Project Groups. *R&D Management, 12*(1), pp. 7–20.

Kleinert, S. and Volkmann, C., 2019. Equity crowdfunding and the role of investor discussion boards. *Venture Capital, 21*(4), pp. 1–26. doi:10.1080/13691066.2019.1569853

Lai, S. and Teo, M., 2008. Home-biased analysts in emerging markets. *Journal of Financial and Quantitative Analysis, 43*(3), pp. 685–716.

Lambert, T. and Schwienbacher, A., 2010. An empirical analysis of crowdfunding. *Social Science Research Network, 1578175*, pp. 1–23.

Lane, P.J. and Lubatkin, M., 1998. Relative absorptive capacity and interorganizational learning. *Strategic Management Journal, 19*(5), pp. 461–477.

Lerner, J., 1995. Venture capitalists and the oversight of private firms. *The Journal of Finance, 50*(1), pp. 301–318.

Li, Y., Vertinsky, I.B. and Li, J., 2014. National distances, international experience, and venture capital investment performance. *Journal of Business Venturing, 29*(4), pp. 471–489.

Lichtenstein, B.M.B. and Brush, C.G., 2001. How do "resource bundles" develop and change in new ventures? A dynamic model and longitudinal exploration. *Entrepreneurship Theory and Practice, 25*(3), pp. 37–58.

Lim, C. and Putnam, R.D., 2010. Religion, social networks, and life satisfaction. *American Sociological Review, 75*(6), pp. 914–933.

Lin, M. and Viswanathan, S., 2015. Home bias in online investments: An empirical study of an online crowdfunding market. *Management Science, 62*(5), pp. 1393–1414.

Liu, Y. and Maula, M., 2016. Local partnering in foreign ventures: Uncertainty, experiential learning, and syndication in cross-border venture capital investments. *Academy of Management Journal, 59*(4), pp. 1407–1429.

Lukkarinen, A., Teich, J.E., Wallenius, H. and Wallenius, J., 2016. Success drivers of online equity crowdfunding campaigns. *Decision Support Systems, 87*, pp. 26–38.

MacMillan, I.C., Kulow, D.M. and Khoylian, R., 1989. Venture capitalists' involvement in their investments: Extent and performance. *Journal of Business Venturing, 4*(1), pp. 27–47.

Mahmood, A., Luffarelli, J. and Mukesh, M., 2019. What's in a logo? The impact of complex visual cues in equity crowdfunding. *Journal of Business Venturing, 34*(1), pp. 41–62.

Miller McPherson, J., Smith-Lovin, L. and Cook, J.M., 2001. Birds of a feather: Homophily in social networks. *Annual Review of Sociology, 27*(1), pp. 415–444.

Mohammadi, A. and Shafi, K., 2018. Gender differences in the contribution patterns of equity-crowdfunding investors. *Small Business Economics, 50*(2), pp. 275–287.

Molina-Morales, F.X., García-Villaverde, P.M. and Parra-Requena, G., 2014. Geographical and cognitive proximity effects on innovation performance in SMEs: A way through knowledge acquisition. *International Entrepreneurship and Management Journal, 10*(2), pp. 231–251.

Mollick, E., 2014. The dynamics of crowdfunding: An exploratory study. *Journal of Business Venturing, 29*(1), pp. 1–16.

Moritz, A., Block, J. and Lutz, E., 2015. Investor communication in equity-based crowdfunding: A qualitative-empirical study. *Qualitative Research in Financial Markets*, 7(3), pp. 309–342.

Nahapiet, J. and Ghoshal, S., 1998. Social capital, intellectual capital, and the organizational advantage. *Academy of Management Review, 23*(2), pp. 242–266.

Nahata, R., Hazarika, S. and Tandon, K., 2014. Success in global venture capital investing: Do institutional and cultural differences matter? *Journal of Financial and Quantitative Analysis, 49*(4), pp. 1039–1070.

Nevin, S., Gleasure, R., O'Reilly, P., Feller, J., Li, S. and Cristoforo, J., 2017, August. Social identity and social media activities in equity crowdfunding. In *Proceedings of the 13th International Symposium on Open Collaboration* (p. 11). ACM.

Nitani, M., Riding, A. and He, B., 2019. On equity crowdfunding: Investor rationality and success factors. *Venture Capital, 21*(2–3), pp. 243–272.

Noseleit, F. and de Faria, P., 2013. Complementarities of internal R&D and alliances with different partner types. *Journal of Business Research, 66*(10), pp. 2000–2006.

Ordanini, A., Miceli, L., Pizzetti, M. and Parasuraman, A., 2011. Crowd-funding: Transforming customers into investors through innovative service platforms. *Journal of Service Management, 22*(4), pp. 443–470.

Penrose, E., 1959. *The Theory of the Growth of the Firm*. John Wiley & Sons, New York.

Piva, E. and Rossi-Lamastra, C., 2018. Human capital signals and entrepreneurs' success in equity crowdfunding. *Small Business Economics, 51*(3), pp. 667–686.

Plummer, L.A., Allison, T.H. and Connelly, B.L., 2016. Better together? Signaling interactions in new venture pursuit of initial external capital. *Academy of Management Journal, 59*(5), pp. 1585–1604.

Politis, D., 2008. Business angels and value added: What do we know and where do we go? *Venture Capital, 10*(2), pp. 127–147.

Presutti, M., Boari, C. and Majocchi, A., 2011. The importance of proximity for the start-ups' knowledge acquisition and exploitation. *Journal of Small Business Management, 49*(3), pp. 361–389.

Ralcheva, A. and Roosenboom, P., 2016. On the road to success in equity crowdfunding. Available at SSRN: https://ssrn.com/abstract=2727742 or http://dx.doi.org/10.2139/ssrn.2727742

Rallet, A. and Torre, A., 1999. Is geographical proximity necessary in the innovation networks in the era of global economy? *GeoJournal, 49*(4), pp. 373–380.

Salter, A., Criscuolo, P. and Ter Wal, A.L., 2014. Coping with open innovation: Responding to the challenges of external engagement in R&D. *California Management Review, 56*(2), pp. 77–94.

Sapienza, H.J., 1992. When do venture capitalists add value? *Journal of Business Venturing*, 7(1), pp. 9–27.

Sapienza, H.J., Manigart, S. and Vermeir, W., 1996. Venture capitalist governance and value added in four countries. *Journal of Business Venturing, 11*(6), pp. 439–469.

Schierjott, I., Brennecke, J. and Rank, O.N., 2018. Entrepreneurial attitudes as drivers of managers' boundary-spanning knowledge ties in the context of high-tech clusters. *Journal of Small Business Management, 56*, pp. 108–131.

Siegel, J.I., Licht, A.N. and Schwartz, S.H., 2011. Egalitarianism and international investment. *Journal of Financial Economics, 102*(3), pp. 621–642.

Signori, A. and Vismara, S., 2016. Returns on investments in equity crowdfunding. https://papers.ssrn.com/sol3/papers.cfm?abstract_id=2765488.

Singh, J.V., Tucker, D.J. and House, R.J., 1986. Organizational legitimacy and the liability of newness. *Administrative Science Quarterly, 31*, pp. 171–193.

Sorenson, O., 2018. Social networks and the geography of entrepreneurship. *Small Business Economics*, *51*(3), pp. 527–537.

Spence, A.M., 1973. Job market signaling. *Quarterly Journal of Economics*, *87*(1973), pp. 355–374.

Stern, P.N., 1980. Grounded theory methodology: Its uses and processes. *Image*, *12*(1), pp. 20–23.

Stinchcombe, A.L., 1965. Organizations and social structure. *Handbook of Organizations*, *44*(2), pp. 142–193.

Strauss, A. and Corbin, J., 1998. *Basics of Qualitative Research Techniques*. Sage Publications, Thousand Oaks, CA.

Strong, N. and Xu, X., 2003. Understanding the equity home bias: Evidence from survey data. *Review of Economics and Statistics*, *85*(2), pp. 307–312.

Thompson, P. and Fox-Kean, M., 2005. Patent citations and the geography of knowledge spillovers: A reassessment. *American Economic Review*, *95*(1), pp. 450–460.

Vismara, S., 2016. Equity retention and social network theory in equity crowdfunding. *Small Business Economics*, *46*(4), pp. 579–590.

Vismara, S., 2018. Information cascades among investors in equity crowdfunding. *Entrepreneurship Theory and Practice*, *42*(3), pp. 467–497.

Vismara, S., 2019. Sustainability in equity crowdfunding. *Technological Forecasting and Social Change*, *141*, pp. 98–106.

Walthoff-Borm, X., Schwienbacher, A. and Vanacker, T., 2018. Equity crowdfunding: First resort or last resort? *Journal of Business Venturing*, *33*(4), pp. 513–533.

Wang, W., Mahmood, A., Sismeiro, C. and Vulkan, N., 2019. The evolution of equity crowdfunding: Insights from co-investments of angels and the crowd. *Research Policy*, *48*(8), p. 103727.

Wassmer, U., 2010. Alliance portfolios: A review and research agenda. *Journal of Management*, *36*(1), pp. 141–171.

West, G.P. and Noel, T.W., 2009. The impact of knowledge resources on new venture performance. *Journal of Small Business Management*, *47*(1), pp. 1–22.

Wiklund, J. and Shepherd, D., 2005. Entrepreneurial orientation and small business performance: A configurational approach. *Journal of Business Venturing*, *20*(1), pp. 71–91.

Wright, M. and Robbie, K., 1998. Venture capital and private equity: A review and synthesis. *Journal of Business Finance & Accounting*, *25*(5 & 6), pp. 521–570.

Wuyts, S. and Dutta, S., 2014. Benefiting from alliance portfolio diversity: The role of past internal knowledge creation strategy. *Journal of Management*, *40*(6), pp. 1653–1674.

Yli-Renko, H., Autio, E. and Sapienza, H.J., 2001. Social capital, knowledge acquisition, and knowledge exploitation in young technology-based firms. *Strategic Management Journal*, *22*(6–7), pp. 587–613.

Ziegler, T., Shneor, R., Wenzlaff, K., Odorović, A., Johanson, D., Hao, R. and Ryll, L., 2019. *4th European Alternative Finance Benchmarking Report*. University of Cambridge, Cambridge Centre for Alternative Finance.

7

EQUITY CROWDFUNDED COMPANIES

Where are they now?

The last chapter in this book examines the long-term benefits to firms that receive crowdfunding. We review the literature on companies or projects that successfully raised funds on crowdfunding platforms, focusing on outcomes and including firm failure, follow-on fundraising, and firm performance. We conduct an empirical analysis of companies that searched for equity crowdfunding and identify some key factors related to their performance including fundraising activities and companies' and founders' characteristics. The chapter concludes by proposing some directions for future research on crowdfunding.

7.1 Equity crowdfunded companies' performance: a review of the literature

Although crowdfunding is a relatively new method of funding, it has become an increasingly relevant means of alternative financing for start-ups and small ventures.

The phenomenon of crowdfunding has been analysed from various perspectives to try to develop a theoretical model that explains the dynamics underlying crowdfunding. As highlighted in Chapter 3 (literature review on crowdfunding), most current academic research on crowdfunding focuses on investigating factors associated with campaign success (e.g. Ahlers et al., 2015; Mollick, 2014; Colombo et al., 2015; Giudici et al., 2018; Vismara, 2016a) and the reasons for choosing equity crowdfunding as a financial instrument (Walthoff-Borm et al., 2018a).

Among the factors identified, scholars have highlighted the importance of project quality (Mollick, 2014; Ahlers et al., 2015; Kgoroeadira et al., 2019), internal social capital (Colombo et al., 2015; Vismara, 2016b; Butticè et al., 2017), geographical proximity (Agrawal et al., 2015; Lin and Viswanathan, 2016), and the characteristics of the geographic location of the project (Giudici et al., 2018; Di Pietro et al., 2018) for promoting crowdfunding project success.

The ultimate goal of crowdfunded companies is to build an enduring business. Therefore, a successful crowdfunding campaign is just the starting point (Signori and Vismara, 2018; Walthoff-Born et al., 2018a). Less research attention has been paid to understanding whether and under what conditions equity crowdfunding of entrepreneurial firms promotes survival, good economic performance, and subsequent access to external capital from traditional professional investors.

A few studies that examine post-equity crowdfunding performance show that entrepreneurs are able to leverage the investor networks generated in the course of the equity crowdfunding campaign (Di Pietro et al., 2018). Crowd investors provide firm founders with two main types of inputs: product, strategy, and market-related knowledge, and ties to networks of industry players and other relevant stakeholders. The Di Pietro et al. (2018) study suggests, also, that start-ups that exploit the crowd network are more likely to be successful two years later compared to start-ups that do not maintain links to their crowd funders.

In research on firm performance following a successful equity crowdfunding campaign, there are a few studies on the relation between crowdfunding and firm outcomes. Signori and Vismara (2018) investigated 212 crowd-backed start-ups in the UK that received funding between 2011 and 2015. They found that 18% of them had failed within two years of receiving the funding, and 35% had been able to raise further funding, although only 9% of these had been financed by traditional investors. Walthoff-Borm et al. (2018a) found that some 30% of firms that raised equity crowdfunding between 2012 and 2015 on Crowdcube had failed by November 2017.

There is a stream of work that examines the effects of crowdfunding on follow-on fundraising from professional investors, such as venture capitalists and business angels, which are two of the most frequent sources of external funding for early stage ventures (Shane, 2012), and they are likely to have implications long after the initial capital is injected.

Hornuf et al. (2018) show that firms that received equity crowdfunding have a higher chance of obtaining follow-on financing from business angels and venture capitalists. Cumming et al. (2019) contribute to the debate by examining the ownership structure of firms seeking equity crowdfunding. They found that a deeper separation between ownership and control rights reduces the likelihood of attracting interest from professional investors.

A recent study by Butticè et al. (2019) looks at the differences between firms funded through Crowdcube and Seedrs, which, respectively, are based on a direct shareholder structure and a nominee structure. The direct shareholder structure allows the crowd investors to become legal shareholders in the business they have supported. In the case of the nominee structure, the crowd is represented by one legal shareholder, that is, the nominee, in the form of the equity crowdfunding platform, which holds and manages the shares of the supported firms on behalf of the investors. Using a unique dataset of 290 firms that successfully raised funds via these two most prominent UK equity crowdfunding portals between 2011 and March 2018, Butticè et al. (2019) show that a successful equity crowdfunding campaign increases the chances of VC financing. This association is stronger for equity crowdfunding campaigns with a nominee shareholder structure. These authors argue that the number of shareholders involved in a direct shareholder structure is a deterrent to professional investors. The difficulty involved in obtaining consents and signatures if several hundred individuals are involved can slow decision-making, resulting in venture capitalists being less keen to invest in direct shareholder structured firms. The nominee shareholder structure avoids the problems associated to dispersed ownership. The entrepreneur needs only to interact with the platform, rather than the entire investor base, which reduces coordination costs (Walthoff-Borm et al., 2018b; Cumming et al., 2019). Also, decision-making is faster if it is managed directly by the platform.

In the context of reward-based crowdfunding, Drover et al. (2017) show that venture capitalists have a greater willingness to conduct due diligence in the case of firms that raised reward-based crowdfunding compared to angel-backed firms. They found no such association for firms that raised equity via crowdfunding. Mödl (2018) used an experimental design and highlights that crowdfunding is considered a negative signal by professional venture capitalists. However, firms that achieved large amounts of reward-based crowdfunding can be attractive for venture capitalists.

The effect of crowdfunding on longer-term firm outcomes, such as financial performance, innovation, and firm growth, seems to have been the most overlooked. However, Walthoff-Borm et al. (2018b) show that UK equity crowdfunded firms achieve less successful financial performance (i.e. return on assets), but are more innovative (i.e. higher intangible assets ratios, and more patent applications and patents granted) than matching UK non-crowdfunded firms.

However, the findings in this literature are far from conclusive and tend to diverge based on platform and type of crowdfunding. Overall, there seems to be relatively consistent evidence that successful reward-based crowdfunding facilitates subsequent receipt of VC. However, for other forms of crowdfunding, such as lending-based or equity-based, there is either no effect or contrasting results.

7.2 Key factors affecting post-crowdfunding company performance: an empirical study

Taking equity crowdfunding as initiating seed financing (Walthoff-Born et al., 2018a), the research in this chapter contributes to the extant literature on post-campaign performance of equity crowdfunded companies by investigating the main factors influencing firm survival and access to additional external finance and other resources.

In this study, we address the following research questions: *How do equity crowdfunded start-ups perform? What are the factors that affect their success?*

Our empirical setting is based on a sample of 213 companies that raised equity capital between 2012 and 2016 on the UK crowdfunding platforms Crowdcube and Seedrs. We used data from Crowdcube, Seedrs, and Crunchbase to construct our dataset, and we tracked the performance of these companies to March 2018. Among our sample of 213 companies, 54% had raised funds via Crowdcube and 46% via Seedrs.

The headquarters of 90% of the firms in our sample are in the UK, with 60% of these 90% having head offices in the city of London. In terms of size, 63% of the companies in the sample employ between 1 and 10 people, 34% have between 11 and 50 employees, and the remaining 3% have more than 51 employees.

The firms are from several sectors – from high-tech to traditional industries such as food and beverages, real estate, finance, and home and personal care. Most of our sample companies were founded between 2010 and 2015; the average age at March 2018 was 6.3 years. On average, the time between year of incorporation and receipt of first investment was 2.4 years.

Our data show that those firms that became involved in crowdfunding within one year after incorporation, registered higher failure rate in March 2018, compared to those companies that received their first round of crowdfunding 2.5 years after incorporation.

Among funding sources, the first investment received by 88% of the sample companies was equity crowdfunding; 4% had been supported by an accelerator or incubator programme; and the remaining 8% had received business angels or venture capital funding.

In the case of subsequent investments, 53% of the companies have received subsequent equity offerings in the form of either private equity injection (8%) or follow-on crowdfunding offering.

The data show that the firms used equity crowdfunding 1.65 times on average, with the first round of crowdfunding achieving £260,000 on average. The average funding provided by professional investors per round was £1.7 million, much higher than crowdfunding amounts. Finally, the average time between receipt of initial equity crowdfunding and receipt of professional investment is around 2 years compared to 1.2 years between first and second rounds of equity crowdfunding.

In terms of firm performance, 89% of the companies in the sample were still operating in March 2018, 9% of the companies closed down after receiving their first round of crowdfunding, 53% had received private equity or follow-on crowdfunding, and 2% of the companies had been acquired by a big firm as a result of their having an innovative business model.

To better understand the determinants of the post-campaign scenario, such as whether companies are still operating, we consider the impact of (i) firm fundraising activity, (ii) firm characteristics, and (iii) firm founders' experience on post-campaign performance. Information related to the firm's fundraising activity were collected from Crunchbase, an online database that provides information on international public and private companies. Data on company characteristics were collected from the crowdfunding platform websites and CrunchBase, and information on about founder characteristics were collected from LinkedIn.

TABLE 7.1 Variables description

Variables	*Description*	
Company status	Whether the company is active (value 1) or has exited (value 0).	Company performance
No. of equity crowdfunding round	No. of equity crowdfunding rounds between 2012 and 2018	Fundraising activity
Timing of first funding round	Time (in years) between incorporation and first funding round	
Platform	Seedrs (value 1) or Crowdcube (value 0)	
Professional investors	Following crowdfunding, presence of a professional investor as a company shareholder (value 1 and 0 otherwise)	
Age	Firm age at March 2018	Company characteristics
Number of employees	No. of employees	
Sector	Firm industry	
Social network	No. of social networks used by the firm, e.g. Twitter, Facebook, LinkedIn	
Country	Country of incorporation	
Founders' industry experience	Work experience of firm founder in the same or a related industry (value 1 and 0 otherwise)	Founder characteristics
Founder education	Firm founder's level of education. Value 1 for higher education (BA or MSc degree), value 2 for PhD or MBA degree, 0 otherwise	
Founder's gender	Captures the gender diversity of the founding team; the variable takes the value 0 for male founder(s), 1 for female and 2 for mixed (male and female founders)	

Table 7.1 presents the variables for the aspects considered in our estimation model.

We run a logistic regression analysis to estimate the impact on firm performance of the variables described in Table 7.1. Specifically, our dependent variable refers to whether or not the company was still operating in March 2018, when we collected our firm performance data.

Table 7.2 presents the results of our analysis.

The analysis shows that engaging in more than one successful crowdfunding round enhances the chances of start-up success. We argue that this is related to the fact that equity crowdfunding performance may validate the project's market potential. Since crowd funders are potential customers, ability to attract a large number of investors or a large number of backers willing to invest large sums, is a signal that the concept is seen as viable and valuable, which can translate into market demand (Vismara, 2016b).

TABLE 7.2 Effect of fundraising activity, firm, and founder characteristics on company performance

	Company performance				
	Coefficient	*Std. error*	*P-value*	*[95% Conf. Interval]*	
No. of equity crowdfunding rounds	1.826	0.732	0.013*	0.390	3.262
Timing of first funding round	1.073	0.356	0.003**	0.374	1.772
Platform	−2.795	0.882	0.002**	−4.525	−1.064
Professional investors	2.907	1.362	0.033*	0.236	5.578
Firm age	−0.856	0.324	0.008**	−1.491	−0.220
No. of employees	−0.779	0.687	0.257	−2.126	0.568
Industry	1.032	0.734	0.160	−0.407	2.472
Social networks	1.174	0.329	0.000***	0.529	1.819
Country	0.457	0.979	0.640	−1.461	2.377
Founder industry experience	0.884	0.903	0.328	−0.887	2.656
Founder education	−0.487	0.548	0.373	−1.562	0.586
Founder gender	−1.017	0.439	0.021*	−1.880	−0.155
cons_	0.71	2.221	0.749	−3.643	5.063
Observations	213				
R^2	0.39				

† $p < 0.1$; $*p < 0.05$; $**p < 0.01$; $***p < 0.001$.

Also, whenever the firm exposes itself to crowd investors, it opens its boundaries to inflows of different types of resources. Notable is that equity crowdfunding campaigns have been shown to provide more than just funding and to contribute knowledge and access to networks (Di Pietro et al., 2018). Crowd investors, in particular, can improve firm outcomes by providing suggestions about and feedback on potential desired products, advising on strategies and providing market knowledge to the target firm. These inputs can contribute to the development and refinement of products, and increase firm growth.

Equity crowd funders, understood as consumers and market representatives, help to provide information on products, competitors, and potential partners. All these benefits help to reduce the uncertainty related typically to young ventures and, thus, can have an effect on firm survival (Brush et al., 2009).

Another factor that has an influence on firm performance is the timing of the first equity investment. The data point to a positive relationship between the time from the firm's year of incorporation and the time of the first investment round, and firm success. In other words, the longer the time from company establishment to first crowdfunding round, the higher the probability of firm survival.

New ventures tend to have scarce resources and entrepreneurs need to focus their time and attention on refining their product or service to signal viability, in order to attract funding and continue to develop. Firm owners need to consolidate their business and operating models, and exploit internal synergies (Henry, 2017). During the early stages of firm development, it is pivotal for firm owners to maintain control and direct the efforts towards the imagined direction, avoiding that multiple external influences may hamper these efforts.

Companies that seek equity crowdfunding at a later stage in their development are likely to have more resources, allowing better exploitation of the crowd to benefit from its knowledge and networks (Di Pietro et al., 2018). Since crowdfunders are potential customers, having an already developed product or service or, at least, a prototype should increase the attractiveness of the firm. Funding obtained, at this stage, will facilitate product testing and adoption and acquisition of further resources.

Platform selection has also been shown to influence funded firms' performance. The platform is the intermediary (Belleflamme et al., 2014) between funders and entrepreneur. The platform manages the fundraising process, from due diligence to close of the fundraising event and, in the case of successful fundraising, the subsequent interactions with crowdfunders (Ahlers et al., 2015). Each platform has particular goals, strategies, and networks of investors (Dushnitsky and Fitza, 2018). They attract "crowds" that differ in their expertise and location, and select among them to identify the type of funder most appropriate for the proposed business (Giudici et al., 2013). Platforms such as Crowdcube, which has a good record of successful firm funding, are able to match firms to a greater number of potential investors. A larger network of potential crowd funders increases the chances for the firm of engagement in multiple successful crowdfunding rounds.

Results confirm that the involvement of professional investors in equity crowdfunding campaigns has a significant impact on firm performance. Professional investors can provide value added to the firm through their positive impact on innovation (Bertoni and Tykvova, 2015; Lerner, 2000), firm growth (Bertoni et al., 2011; Puri and Zarutskie, 2012), overall economic performance (Colombo and Murtinu, 2017; Chemmanur et al., 2011; Croce et al., 2013), and successful IPO (Chemmanur et al., 2009; Cumming et al., 2017; Puri and Zarutskie, 2012).

Interestingly, also the use of different social network influence funded firms' performance. Good digital visibility can increase the visibility of the firm in the market, which can translate into a higher number of new customers.

7.2.1 Research insights and contributions

The entrepreneur's goal is to build a successful business and studies of how crowdfunding can influence the development of enduring business after fundraising are recent (for a review, see Vanacker et al., 2019). Work assessed the performance of crowd-backed companies based on survival rates (Signori and Vismara, 2018; Walthoff-Borm et al., 2018a), financial performance (Walthoff-Borm et al., 2018b), access to follow-on financing from professional investors (see, e.g. Drover et al., 2017; Cumming et al., 2019; Hornuf et al., 2018), and the platform shareholder structure (Butticè et al., 2019).

Adding to existing studies, among the determinants of the post-campaign scenario, in our study of 213 companies that sought funding on the UK's largest crowdfunding platforms, we find that: (i) companies that sought crowdfunding multiple time had a higher probability of survival; (ii) the length of time between firm establishment and first crowdfunding is an important determinant of later start-up success – companies that received funding later had a higher probability of survival; (iii) the platform and the platform characteristics have an influence on the crowd-backed company's performance; (iv) the presence of professional investors increases the chances of firm survival; and (v) the firm's social network exposure has an effect on survival.

7.3 Research on crowdfunding: reflections and future directions

The existing research on crowdfunding – and equity crowdfunding, in particular, – discusses various aspects of the phenomenon and offers some implications for practice and policy.

The contributions from the research presented in this book correspond to different fundraising phases (see Chapters 3 and 6 for reviews of the literature). Stage 1 can be described as the precursor to crowdfunding. Several studies investigate entrepreneurs' motivations for approaching crowdfunding and the financial and non-financial reasons that lead backers and investors to support innovative projects (see, e.g., Gerber et al., 2012).

Stage 2 refers to the actual fundraising, and the literature examines those factors influencing fundraising and discusses some strategies for increasing fundraising success. This body of work provides a better understanding of what the crowd values and, therefore, how the entrepreneur could tailor the campaign to attract more funds (see, e.g. Mollick, 2014; Vismara, 2016b; Ahlers et al., 2015; Lukkarinen et al., 2016; Mahmood et al., 2019; Bapna, 2017; and see Mochkabadi and Volkmann, 2018 for a review).

Stage 3 refers to the post-fundraising phase. Chapter 7 shows that scholars have only recently started to investigate the long-term benefits of crowdfunding for new ventures (see e.g. Signori and Vismara, 2018; Vanacker et al., 2019; Drover et al., 2017; Walthoff-Borm et al., 2018b; Butticè et al., 2019). There is evidence about how crowd-backed companies perform and the factors that influence their performance including the characteristics of the crowdfunding platform, its network of investors, and the platform's shareholder structure (Butticè et al., 2019). This research has important implications for practice. Entrepreneurs should consider the long-term impact of the platform's shareholder structure when choosing which crowdfunding platform to use to raise funding. They should choose a platform whose ownership structure fits their financing plan or implement strategies to mitigate potential follow-on investors' concerns.

Future work could provide a better understanding of the long-term benefits and disadvantages of crowdfunding by more detailed investigation of the performance of crowd-backed companies. It is important to consider innovation activity, firm growth, and potential for expansion into new markets, to assess the economic impact of crowdfunding on the national economy.

Current crowdfunding research is mainly focused on US-based and UK-based platforms, but there are hundreds of other crowdfunding platforms worldwide (Ziegler et al., 2018a, 2018b). More research is needed, to validate or reject the existing findings by investigating platforms in different countries. A cross-country sample would allow examination of the role of the platform and the effect of country characteristics on the performance of crowd-funded companies.

A more detailed understanding is needed of how the crowd contributes to firm performance. This would require a study of the relationship between entrepreneur and crowd investors and the non-financial benefits investors provide (Di Pietro et al., 2018). This would include examination of which types of firms are able to capture more value added from their crowd funders, and why. This research should address the following research questions: What are the barriers to the exploitation of the crowd's expertise? How can the entrepreneurial team capture the non-financial benefits that can be provided by the crowd? How can entrepreneurs leverage the crowd's expertise and increase its contribution to firm performance?

Finally, future research could look at cross-country and cross-regional differences in the development of crowdfunding around the world, both in terms of number of platforms and investment transactions. There is significant variation in the adoption of crowdfunding across countries (Ziegler et al., 2018a). Differences could be related to the development of formal institutions such as legal frameworks and informal institutions such as culture, although evidence is limited.

References

Agrawal, A., Catalini, C. and Goldfarb, A., 2015. Crowdfunding: Geography, social networks, and the timing of investment decisions. *Journal of Economics & Management Strategy*, *24*(2), pp. 253–274.

Ahlers, G.K., Cumming, D., Günther, C. and Schweizer, D., 2015. Signaling in equity crowdfunding. *Entrepreneurship Theory and Practice*, *39*(4), pp. 955–980.

Bapna, S. 2017. Complementarity of signals in early-stage equity investment decisions: Evidence from a randomized field experiment. *Management Science*, *65*(2), pp. 933–952.

Belleflamme, P., Lambert, T. and Schwienbacher, A., 2014. Crowdfunding: Tapping the right crowd. *Journal of Business Venturing*, *29*(5), pp. 585–609.

Bertoni, F., Colombo, M.G. and Grilli, L., 2011. Venture capital financing and the growth of high-tech start-ups: Disentangling treatment from selection effects. *Research Policy*, *40*(7), pp. 1028–1043.

Bertoni, F. and Tykvová, T., 2015. Does governmental venture capital spur invention and innovation? Evidence from young European biotech companies. *Research Policy*, *44*(4), pp. 925–935.

Brush, C.G., Ceru, D.J. and Blackburn, R., 2009. Pathways to entrepreneurial growth: The influence of management, marketing, and money. *Business Horizons*, *52*(5), pp. 481–491.

Butticè, V., Colombo, M.G. and Wright, M., 2017. Serial crowdfunding, social capital, and project success. *Entrepreneurship Theory and Practice*, *41*(2), pp. 183–207.

Butticè, V., Di Pietro, F. and Tenca, F. 2019. Is equity crowdfunding always good? The role of deal structure in influencing entrepreneurs' ability to attract professional investors. *Working Paper Presented at the 4th Entrepreneurial Conference*, Trier, Germany.

Chemmanur, T.J., He, S. and Nandy, D.K., 2009. The going-public decision and the product market. *The Review of Financial Studies*, *23*(5), pp. 1855–1908.

Chemmanur, T.J., Krishnan, K. and Nandy, D.K., 2011. How does venture capital financing improve efficiency in private firms? A look beneath the surface. *The Review of Financial Studies*, *24*(12), pp. 4037–4090.

Colombo, M.G., Franzoni, C. and Rossi–Lamastra, C., 2015. Internal social capital and the attraction of early contributions in crowdfunding. *Entrepreneurship Theory and Practice*, *39*(1), pp. 75–100.

Colombo, M.G. and Murtinu, S., 2017. Venture capital investments in Europe and portfolio firms' economic performance: Independent versus corporate investors. *Journal of Economics & Management Strategy*, *26*(1), pp. 35–66.

Croce, A., Martí, J. and Murtinu, S., 2013. The impact of venture capital on the productivity growth of European entrepreneurial firms: "Screening" or "value added" effect? *Journal of Business Venturing*, *28*(4), pp. 489–510.

Cumming, D., Meoli, M. and Vismara, S., 2019. Investors' choices between cash and voting rights: Evidence from dual-class equity crowdfunding. *Research Policy*, *48*(8), pp. 2–19.

Cumming, D.J., Grilli, L. and Murtinu, S., 2017. Governmental and independent venture capital investments in Europe: A firm-level performance analysis. *Journal of Corporate Finance*, *42*, pp. 439–459.

Di Pietro, F., Prencipe, A. and Majchrzak, A., 2018. Crowd equity investors: An underutilized asset for open innovation in startups. *California Management Review*, *60*(2), pp. 43–70.

Drover, W., Wood, M.S. and Zacharakis, A., 2017. Attributes of angel and crowdfunded investments as determinants of VC screening decisions. *Entrepreneurship Theory and Practice*, *41*(3), pp. 323–347.

Dushnitsky, G. and Fitza, M.A., 2018. Are we missing the platforms for the crowd? Comparing investment drivers across multiple crowdfunding platforms. *Journal of Business Venturing Insights*, *10*, p. e00100.

Gerber, E.M., Hui, J.S. and Kuo, P.Y., 2012, February. Crowdfunding: Why people are motivated to post and fund projects on crowdfunding platforms. In *Proceedings of the International Workshop on Design, Influence, and Social Technologies: Techniques, Impacts and Ethics* (Vol. 2, No. 11, p. 10). Northwestern University, Evanston, IL.

Giudici, G., Guerini, M. and Rossi Lamastra, C., 2013. Crowdfunding in Italy: State of the art and future prospects. *Economia e Politica Industriale-Journal of Industrial and Business Economics*, *40*(4), pp. 173–188.

Giudici, G., Guerini, M. and Rossi-Lamastra, C., 2018. Reward-based crowdfunding of entrepreneurial projects: The effect of local altruism and localized social capital on proponents' success. *Small Business Economics*, *50*(2), pp. 307–324.

Henry, P., 2017. Why some startups succeed (and why most fail). *Entrepreneur*, 18 February.

Hornuf, L., Schmitt, M. and Stenzhorn, E., 2018. Equity crowdfunding in Germany and the United Kingdom: Follow-up funding and firm failure. *Corporate Governance: An International Review*, *26*(5), pp. 331–354.

Kgoroeadira, R., Burke, A. and van Stel, A., 2019. Small business online loan crowdfunding: Who gets funded and what determines the rate of interest? *Small Business Economics*, *52*(1), pp. 67–87.

Lerner, J., 2000. Assessing the contribution of venture capital. *The RAND Journal of Economics*, *31*(4), pp. 674–692.

Lin, M. and Viswanathan, S., 2016. Home bias in online investments: An empirical study of an online crowdfunding market. *Management Science*, *62*(5), pp. 1393–1414.

Lukkarinen, A., Teich, J.E., Wallenius, H. and Wallenius, J., 2016. Success drivers of online equity crowdfunding campaigns. *Decision Support Systems*, *87*, pp. 26–38.

Mahmood, A., Luffarelli, J. and Mukesh, M., 2019. What's in a logo? The impact of complex visual cues in equity crowdfunding. *Journal of Business Venturing*, *34*(1), pp. 41–62.

Mochkabadi, K. and Volkmann, C.K., 2018. Equity crowdfunding: A systematic review of the literature. *Small Business Economics*, pp. 1–44.

Mödl, M., 2018. Is wisdom of the crowd a positive signal? Effects of crowdfinancing on subsequent venture capital selection. Available at https://papers.ssrn.com/sol3/papers.cfm?abstract_id=3222461.

Mollick, E., 2014. The dynamics of crowdfunding: An exploratory study. *Journal of Business Venturing*, *29*(1), pp. 1–16.

Puri, M. and Zarutskie, R., 2012. On the life cycle dynamics of venture-capital-and non-venture-capital-financed firms. *The Journal of Finance*, *67*(6), pp. 2247–2293.

Shane, S., 2012. The importance of angel investing in financing the growth of entrepreneurial ventures. *The Quarterly Journal of Finance*, *2*(2), p. 1250009.

Signori, A. and Vismara, S., 2018. Does success bring success? The post-offering lives of equity-crowdfunded firms. *Journal of Corporate Finance*, *50*, pp. 575–591.

Vanacker, T., Vismara, S. and Walthoff-Borm, X., 2019. What happens after a crowdfunding campaign? In Landström, H., Parhankangas, A. and Mason, C. (eds.), *Handbook of Research on Crowdfunding*, p. 227. Edward Elgar Publishing, Cheltenham, UK.

Vismara, S., 2016a. Equity retention and social network theory in equity crowdfunding. *Small Business Economics*, *46*(4), pp. 579–590.

Vismara, S., 2016b. Information cascades among investors in equity crowdfunding. *Entrepreneurship Theory and Practice*, *42*(3), pp. 467–497.

Walthoff-Borm, X., Vanacker, T.R. and Collewaert, V., 2018b. Equity crowdfunding, shareholder structures, and firm performance. *Corporate Governance: An International Review*, *26*(5), pp. 314–330.

Walthoff-Borm, X., Schwienbacher, A. and Vanacker, T., 2018a. Equity crowdfunding: First resort or last resort? *Journal of Business Venturing*, *33*(4), pp. 513–533.

Ziegler, T., Johanson, D., King, M., Zhang, B., Mammadova, L., Ferri, F., Trappe, R., Suresh, K., Hao, R., Ryll, L. and Yerolemou, K., 2018a. *Reaching New Heights: The 3rd Americas Alternative Finance Industry Report*. University of Cambridge, Cambridge Centre for Alternative Finance, Cambridge, UK.

Ziegler, T., Shneor, R., Wenzlaff, K., Odorović, A., Johanson, D., Hao, R. and Ryll, L., 2018b. *Shifting Paradigms. The 4th European Alternative Finance Benchmarking Report*. University of Cambridge, Cambridge Centre for Alternative Finance, Cambridge, UK.

INDEX

Note: Page numbers in italic and bold refers to figures and table, respectively.
Page numbers followed by n refers to notes.